BUSINESS
IN THE TIME OF
CORONA

How to Pivot
**Your Career or Startup and
Succeed in Disruption**

SAM KAMANI

CONTENTS

PREFACE

*"Hope is important because it
can make the present moment
less difficult to bear. If we believe
that tomorrow will be better,
we can bear hardship today."*
- THICH NHAT HANH

Introduction

I wrote this book for the person who feels stuck
between a rock and a hard place. I wrote this book
because I want to uplift and build people up.
Especially when they are going through dark times.

Economic strife, sickness, negativity in the media,
and isolation can all take their toll, making people
anxious and depressed around the world. That is why
I wanted to share the strategies that have worked for
me when I have gone through challenging times in
my life.

Throughout the book I also share short stories of other entrepreneurs, founders, startups, and companies, who have successfully turned their fortunes around for the better. Many started or experienced growth during downturns.

I do not underestimate your challenges and situation; everyone has their own battles that they are fighting. I have empathy for your situation. You might be pushing a 10-ton boulder up Mount Everest. Maybe you are coming across challenges that you have never faced before. That's why I wrote this book, to equip you with the tools necessary to find a better way ahead.

If this book can provide hope and positivity to even one person, then this book has done its job, and all my late nights and hard work have been worth it.

In this book I will provide you with step-by-step practical strategies on how to overcome fear and worry when you are going through disruptive times.

Pivot

A large part of this book focuses on pivoting. This book will take you through case studies of how some startups and businesses have overcome disruption by pivoting.

I will break down in detail how you can perform a pivot regardless of the size of your company or organization. And what the secret ingredients are that make a successful pivot.

In this book, I share things that I wish I could tell myself 20 years ago, like how to pivot your career or startup with no money.

Persist

This book will also delve into the value of having Grit for your career or business. It will answer the following question:

When should you persist instead of pivoting? I'll also share examples of people and companies that have persisted despite the odds.

Survive and Thrive

When a pivot is done right, your career or startup will attain new heights. This will also examine the topic of innovation and what role innovation plays in pivots.

Practice what you preach

I have always been fascinated with the idea of pivots and why some startups can successfully pivot and reinvent themselves, whereas other larger organizations, with much more resources, are unable to do that.

I started writing this book in Jan 2020. Initially, I was only going to write about Pivoting your startup or career, and knowing when you should pivot and when you should persist.

By the end of March 2020, over 3 billion people around the world were in lockdown. For me, it took a couple of weeks for the gravity of the situation to set in. As soon as I realized the impact this event was going to have, I immediately wanted to help.

In mid-April 2020, I decided to **pivot** my book to help businesses and individuals who are facing the adverse effect of Covid-19. I quickly executed my pivot once I had decided that this book should launch on Amazon Kindle and print before the end of May 2020.

The last book I co-authored, "The 30 Day Startup", is downloaded thousands of times every month in places where English is not the first language.

That's why I have written this book in an easy-to-read language with a conversational tone.

You do not need any existing technical knowledge to read this; it is extremely light on jargon.

Reading this book will have a transformative effect on your career, business, and your life!

EVERYTHING IS TERRIBLE

- The purpose of this book is to bring you hope and help you see the light at the end of the tunnel.
- I want to show you how you can take back control of your life regardless of the state of the economy.

Y ou might be reading this while the world is still in the middle of a pandemic, or maybe when pandemic, social distancing, and daily death tolls are nothing more than just a distant memory. I am starting the book with my own experience and observation during the Covid-19 lockdown in New Zealand.

My personal experience

It was Monday, March 23rd 2020; I went to work as usual. It didn't take me much time to get to work as quite a few people had already started working from home. I work from a co-working office space in Auckland, New Zealand.

In New Zealand, around midday every day, our Prime Minister announces what actions are being taken to curb coronavirus.

At work everybody expected tighter restrictions to be announced on March 23rd. My colleagues and I expected that the government would announce slightly tighter restrictions. However, our Prime Minister announced a state of emergency and complete lockdown of New Zealand within 48 hours.

Everyone I worked with was in shock. No one expected this to happen in New Zealand. Thoughts of uncertainty ran through everyone's mind. Most didn't even understand what lockdown meant.

Everyone working at the co-working space looked down and depressed. Especially the people who worked for the co-working space. Most co-working spaces in this part of the world were not profitable even before the coronavirus pandemic. During a lockdown, no one would be able to use the co-working space even if they wanted to.

Unlike other long term commercial property leases, co-working spaces do not have long term contracts with their tenants. If tenants cannot use the co-working space, they just stop paying, they do not have to worry about contracts. This would put immense pressure on co-working offices and commercial real estate. This announcement of lockdown meant that many co-working spaces around the world would not survive.

The fear on the face of the receptionist at the co-working space was evident. She was trying very hard to hide her tears. She told me —

"The only thing that scares me is how will I pay my apartment's rent? Everything else I can manage."

She wasn't the only one at the co-working space going through emotional and mental turmoil. Everyone that I know at my co-working office was playing out all the worst-case scenarios in their mind.

After the lockdown announcement, everyone started packing their stuff to take home. I stopped to have a chat with a few more founders who looked shaken to the core.

I remember talking to this young founder of a new digital marketing agency. She said after months of hard work and planning, they had organized the launch party for their new digital agency. This launch party was supposed to happen on Thursday, and the government had just announced a nationwide lockdown to start on Wednesday at midnight. She didn't know if she could get a refund on the event's costs, cancel all the catering, and if her digital marketing agency would even be needed in the post lockdown world.

Every person packing up their things in that co-working space had a story of their own. Everyone was battling their own demons of uncertainty in their mind.

On my way home, I went to my local gym to request them to stop my membership fees. This gym had just opened two months before the lockdown. The gym informed me that everyone's membership was put on hold, and no one would be charged until gyms were allowed to open.

The gym owner shared with me that they were not sure how to keep paying rent and the staff.

It was the same story with the takeaway I visited after the gym. Every single business or person I met had some uncertainty of how they would provide for their families.

And once one business fails, then every other business associated with that business also starts to struggle. We live in an extremely interconnected world. No business is an island. The world of business is more like a food chain dependent on each other instead of a rock that can exist in isolation without much change.

The bigger picture

Apart from my personal experience and interactions on that day, If you look at the news, it feels like this is the end of the world as we know it.

For example, travel and tourism industries have been hit incredibly hard. Most airlines have canceled 85–90% of their flights. Even in good times, the airline business is not known for its high profit margins. Profitability has always been paper-thin throughout the airline industry. That's why history is littered with examples of major airline failures.

Airlines never expected to operate in an environment where 90% of their flights would be cancelled. They still have to pay the lease on equipment, loan payments, bond payments, payroll, and so on.

Most airlines are going to be completely reliant on government handouts and will also accumulate large amounts of debt.

It doesn't get any better for the other industries that rely on air travel, such as the hotel industry. If people cannot get to a destination, you will have nearly no occupancy. Especially if your hotel is on an island. Or if you have a small tourism-related business that relies heavily on tourists coming from overseas.

And every business physically located near an airport is suffering, whether it is food, events, catering, or engineering firms operating in that industry.

As soon as one industry is affected, it creates a domino effect and takes down ten other industries supporting it.

This story is repeated in industry after industry. There isn't a single business or person on this planet that isn't affected by the doom and gloom. Even if their own job is safe, they personally know others who have been affected.

So where is the silver lining?

If everything is so bleak, then what should you do? How do you get to the other side? Moments of change are always filled with uncertainty and doubt. But at the same time, there are plenty of hidden opportunities. When the dust settles, great fortunes will be made, and the people who have managed to adapt by pivoting will be in prime position to exploit all the new opportunities.

OVERCOMING THIS DOWNTURN

*"Change is the law of life. And those
who look only to the past or present
are certain to miss the future."*
—*John F. Kennedy*

Perils of unexpected change

You are playing poker with your friends, having a great time, drinking a 12-year-old single malt whiskey, smoking a cigar. You have the biggest pile of chips because you won the last three rounds. Your mates are distracted and talking about how their favorite sports team is going to do well this year. You are completely immersed in this social experience and having a great time.

Next time the cards are dealt, you are mostly thinking about which cards you will be dealt, and how your friends are going to respond to their cards. You are trying to read the room and plan your next move. You are thinking that either you will win or lose based on the rules of Texas Holdem Poker. The possibilities of the moves that people make are limited to the players' skills and the rules.

The Covid-19 situation we are now in is akin to having all the rules of your game changed suddenly, unexpectedly and completely. Imagine, the next time the cards are dealt, there is an earthquake which leads to a power cut. When the lights turn back on, everything has changed. All your chips and friends you were playing with are gone. They are replaced with a computer and some virtual players. You don't even know if they are human or computer-generated bots. Your poker chips have turned into digital currencies. These digital currencies are on a timer; if you do not use them, then they are returned to the bank or house. The rules have changed, and you are required to play the game, otherwise you will lose all your chips and pay accumulated debt.

How are you going to react? Are you going to fall back on the old rules of Texas Holdem Poker and lose everything, or are you going to play this new game to the best of your ability?

Suppose you choose to act how you have always acted. You say to yourself, "I have always played the game like this and often win. So I will continue to play the game in the same way. I will ignore the digital currencies timer and the fact that I might be playing against algorithms."

Alternatively, you decide to accept that the game has changed forever. You move quickly to figure out how things work now and find out that, in fact, you can borrow a lot more money when it is in the form of virtual chips. This allows you to make bigger, bolder bets. Also, you rapidly learn that the algorithms behave in certain ways, and real players behave differently. You start putting all this new-found knowledge to good use.

Also, you realize that the rules have not only changed for you but for all the players. So you want to be the first one that adapts to the new rules of playing and start winning the game.

Similar to my fictitious example above, the rules of the game have suddenly changed due to Covid-19. Covid-19 has suddenly become the world's largest

Chief Technology Officer bringing digital transformation to the whole planet. For most businesses and individuals, this will pose a question.

Are you going to stick to your old ways? Or are you going to pivot your business or career to win in the new paradigm? If you do not make a choice and decide to wait then, that is also a choice. That means you have chosen to be at the mercy of the environment around you.

However, making a choice to pivot is easier said than done. Career or business pivots are never easy to make. They are especially hard when all your resources are already stretched to the max.

Past experience with major downturns

Our generation isn't the first one to go through downturns. Pandemics, Recessions, Depressions, War, and major natural calamities have happened throughout the past.

And every time our planet goes through such a major event, it brings forth a whole range of disruptions.

These disruptions, in return, give rise to new professions, businesses, and ways of living. Those businesses and professions that cannot pivot and adapt fast enough are lost to the history books.

One such example is of Walt and Roy Disney. In 1928, they introduced the world to Mickey Mouse via their short-animated feature Steamboat Willie. About one year after that, the duo incorporated Walt Disney Productions, and the Great Depression started. The brothers knew that whenever there are troubling times, people look for cheaper entertainment. They had the insight to foresee that America needed a smile more than ever before. Ninety years later, Disney is a behemoth with over 200,000 employees and a market cap north of US$190 Billion.

Disney is not the only outlier. Every recession, depression, or downturn forces people and organizations to think outside the box.

But what if you do not want to start a new business?

Or

What if you already owned a business before this downturn?

Or

What if you just launched your company, and this disruption arrived?

You still won't be the first person or first generation to go through this.

Salesforce, Google, and Facebook - though they didn't start during the Covid-19 disruption - were all launched right before major economic meltdowns. Google (1998) and Salesforce (1999) right before the dot-com bubble burst, and Facebook (2004) shortly before the Global Financial Crisis.

They all had to adapt and change their business models.

Facebook' Chief Operating Officer - Sheryl Sandberg had just joined the company before the 2008 Recession. Over a decade later Business Insider interviewed her in April 2020 to find out about her experience in helping a startup navigate recession.

She explained: *"We had a very small business and we were worried."* Sandberg further pointed to a crucial question the company's leadership had to ask itself: *"What is your core business, and what is the core service you're providing?"*

So what did Facebook do?

Facebook was forced to adapt to the conditions. The core part of Facebook's business in 2007/8 was advertising. They had to pivot their ad products and pricing strategy to work for that moment.

They could have said; no, we will continue doing what has worked for the last four years; the recession is going to be over soon. However, they took a more proactive approach and decided to pivot and adapt. The rest is history.

When the GFC was over, Facebook was in a prime position to take advantage of better economic conditions. Lots of other blogs, news websites, social, and networking websites didn't survive the GFC.

Facebook decided to learn the rules of the new game and played it well. This wasn't the last time Facebook would have to learn the new rules of the game or learn a completely new game. Regardless of whether you think Facebook is an ethical or unethical business, you have to admit the effectiveness of its leadership. Facebook's leadership has managed to drag it out of multiple storms and has shown its resilience.

Conclusion

The Covid-19 situation is going to disrupt how things are done. It will present you with a choice — pivot, adapt, and prosper or resist change, struggle, and perish.

Most of the people I know and talk with in business, and enterprising entrepreneurs, want to move forward and adapt to the new world.

And I am sure you are also looking for ways to make the best of this horrible situation or some other challenging situation in the future, otherwise you would not be reading this book.

Before we tackle how to pivot and grab those opportunities, I want to share my perspective on why it is so hard to grab opportunities in a downturn, why people feel powerless, and what stops them from taking action.

LOSING CONTROL

"People have a hard time letting
go of their suffering. Out of a
fear of the unknown, they prefer
suffering that is familiar."
- Nhat Hanh

As per the previous chapter:
If you know that to overcome this down-turn, you need to pivot and adapt to the new sets of rules, why is it so hard to take action?

What makes us procrastinate and stops us from adapting to the new environment?

I believe that it is because of fear of losing perceived control. You spend years and decades formulating your life, and suddenly you are pushed into the complete unknown.

You start believing that if you do X, it will lead to Y.

For example, if you go to school and do well, you will get into a good university, which will lead to a better paying job. This will lead to getting a mortgage and owning a house. Or you might start a business instead of going through the education and job route, which you expect will bring prosperity to you. For hundreds of millions of people around the world, this is what happens more or less. School -> university -> job -> house -> family etc…

Nowhere in plans like this, are there any expectations of a once in a 100-year event, that we are going through right now. You suddenly feel like the rug has been pulled out from under your feet. You just want to scream, "this is not supposed to happen." You feel that all your plans are ruined.

In reality, you never had that much control. You just cannot dictate when the next earthquake will happen. Or when the next supervolcano will blow up and cover the planet in dark clouds for two years, causing global famine. Or when there will be a pandemic larger than bubonic plague.

Just like in card games, you cannot control what cards are dealt to you or how your opponents play; you can only control the way you play them. For most people around the world, this is the first time they have realized that life can deal you a good hand or a bad hand. And this realization that you never controlled the thing you thought you did can be terrifying.

According to Psychology Today magazine — one of the most prevalent fears people have is that of losing control. This is the fear that if you don't manage to control the outcome of future events, something terrible will happen.

The crux of the problem is the demand for certainty in a world that is always tentative and uncertain. It is precisely this unrealistic demand that creates the anxiety. You think that you *must* accurately predict and manage the future, not just have some probabilistic and uncertain handle on it.

So what do you do when you start feeling anxious, and you feel like you don't have control over anything.

I am not going to say, "Stop worrying," because that doesn't work. The first thing is to understand that this fear is real; you are not alone; millions around the world are also feeling just like you are.

Here is the system that I use to help me overcome this fear and worry. I call it the OLEG system.

O - Optimism
L - Limitations
E - Ephemeral
G - Goals

Optimism

Even more so than a virus or a pandemic, there is one thing that is even more contagious. It is ideas whether they are positive or negative. Just as Covid-19 used the modern technology of airplanes to transport itself to every corner of the planet, ideas these days use online technology such as social media to rapidly transmit themselves to scores of people.

> *"Optimism is essential to achievement
> and it is also the foundation
> of courage and true progress."*
> *- Nicholas Murray Butler*

Optimism and pessimism are contagious. If you hang out with people who are really optimistic, then you start becoming more optimistic. If you spend a lot of time with negative people, then that is sure to bring you down. You start seeing the world through their lens. I am sure you would have heard this statement before, "*Show me who your friends are, and I'll show you your future.*" I completely agree with this statement.

That's why I believe that during this crisis, you should find positive people to hang out with. It is not only limited to your friend circle. This also applies to what you read and listen to. Some people have this innate ability to fill you with positivity and hope.

This is more pertinent in the age of social media. Are you following people online who are positive, or are you engrossed in reading about conspiracy theories and fake news?

Limitations

Understand the limitations. There are some things that are in your control; however, some things are beyond your or anyone's control. Try to understand your own limitations about what you can and cannot do.

For example, you cannot control if it will rain today or not; however, you can control if you take your umbrella with you.

According to the Greek Stoic Philosopher Epictetus - "*We actually control very little. We don't control what happens to us, we can't control what the people around us say or do, and we can't even fully control our own bodies, which get damaged and sick and ultimately die without regard for our preferences. The only thing that we really control is how we think about things, the judgments we make about things."*

Over the years, I have strived to adopt this philosophy in my day to day living. This is the flowchart of the mental process that I try and go through when I am feeling frustrated.

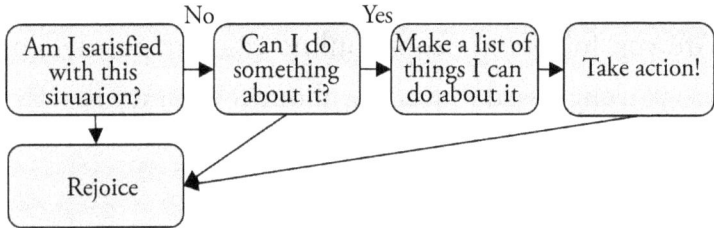

As an example, I would like to share my personal story. When I was running a nutraceutical business, after seven years of being in that industry, I started to become unsatisfied. I wanted to work with products that were more scalable. Software, by its very nature, is extremely scalable compared to a physical product in the nutraceutical niche.

Also, physical products have real-world limitations such as expiry dates, lead time for manufacturing, supply chain issues, complex regulations etc.

There are nearly 190 countries in the world, and every country has its own unique regulation and complexity when dealing with a physical product. I realized that this is something that is beyond my control. If I wanted to negotiate all that, it would take me multiple years and deep pockets.

However, if I have a virtual product or service, then it can scale exponentially throughout the world in a very short period of time.

So I made a list of options for myself outlining what I could do.

1. Exit the current nutraceutical business
2. Remain part-owner and dabble in another business part-time
3. Spend time and energy in upskilling myself
4. Raise money and spend the next 15 years growing the nutraceutical company globally

I weighed the pros and cons of each option and decided to go ahead with number 1.

Embrace the ephemeral

Most things in life do not last forever. Whether it is the Spanish flu or coronavirus, it is not going to last forever. I find this knowledge that everything is temporary, extremely liberating.

When I was growing up, my mom used to read me "Akbar-Birbal" stories. **Akbar-Birbal Stories** were very popular in India during the 1980s and 90s.

There was a Mogul Emperor in India, **Akbar The Great** (1542-1605). He ruled India from 1560 to 1605. He himself was illiterate, but he invited several learned people to his court. Among these people, nine were very famous and were called **Nav Ratna** (nine jewels of the Mogul Crown) of his court.

1. Tansen ... A Great Singer
2. Dasvant ... A Great Painter
3. King Todarmal ... A Financial Wizard
4. Abdu us-Samad ... A Brilliant Calligrapher and Designer of Imperil Coins
5. Abul Fazal ... A Great Historian (whose brother was Faizi)
6. Faizi ... A Great Poet
7. Mir Fareh-ullah Shirazi ... Financier, Philosopher, Physician & Astronomer
8. King Maan Singh ... A Great Man known for His Chivalry
9. Birbal ... A Great Man known for His Valuable Advice

Birbal (1528-1583) is surely one of the most popular figures in Indian history. Birbal's duties in Akbar's court were mostly administrative and military, but he was a very close friend of Akbar too because Akbar loved his wisdom, wit, and subtle humor. He was a minister in the administration of the Mogul Emperor Akbar and one of the members of the inner council of nine advisors. He was also a poet and an author.

The exchanges between Akbar and Birbal have been recorded in many volumes. Many of these have become folk stories in Indian tradition.

One such short story is when Akbar asked Birbal, "Tell me a sentence that: If we read in Happy times we become Sad & if we read in Sad times, we become Happy."

Birbal replied, "This too shall Pass."

Birbal understood the ephemeral nature of life and that change is inevitable. Whether you win the lottery or lose your business to debt, the respective highs and lows from such events are also going to pass. Just like 99.99% of all social media posts, nearly all moments in life are ephemeral.

Goals

Making goals and resolutions are great. There is only one problem with them, and that is that most people fail to achieve most of their goals.

It is not due to a lack of discipline or hard work. It is because most people do not make good goals.

For years I made goals and resolutions that I never achieved because I would write them down in a notepad at the start of the year and forget about them within a few days or weeks. When I wouldn't reach my goals, I would get discouraged and start believing that making goals doesn't work.

Over time I learned that there are two key things I need to do to achieve my goals.

1. Break a larger goal down into smaller goals.
2. Break down the small goals into habits.

For example:

1. If I want to write a book this year, then I will divide it into three key ideas or sections. I will further divide each section into chapters.
2. I will block out two hours every weekday in my calendar to write my book. When I start

doing the same thing every day at the same time, it becomes a habit.

So next time you have a huge goal for your career or your business, divide it into smaller goals, and form habits around actionable tasks.

Conclusion

It is natural to feel fearful or anxious in times of change and disruption. Use the OLEG system to Pivot and Adapt your business or career to the new environment. Surround yourself with optimists, understand your limitations, and work only on what you have the power to change. Accept that everything is ephemeral, and this tough time shall pass. Finally, set goals that you can convert into habits.

In the next chapter, we will look deeper into what is a Pivot and how to Pivot.

WHAT IS A PIVOT?

A **pivot** usually occurs when a company makes a
fundamental change to its **business** after deter-
mining that its product isn't meeting the needs
of their market.

The creator of Humans of New York, Brandon
Stanton, made a fundamental change to his life's direction when he felt that his finance skills weren't needed.

According to Eric Ries, the father of "The Lean
Startup" movement, a pivot is *"A structured course correc-
tion designed to test a new fundamental hypothesis about the
product, strategy, and engine of growth."*

*Over the course of this book, I will take you through
some case studies of successful pivots and give advice on*

how to pivot your business, career or life to succeed in uncertain times.

But first, let's look at the most common types of pivot.

It is possible to pivot in many different ways. When most people think of pivots, they only think about tweaking their product slightly or, in many cases, just changing their distribution; for example, going online instead of offline. However, a pivot to revive your business can take many forms.

Most pivots can be categorized into one of the following four categories.

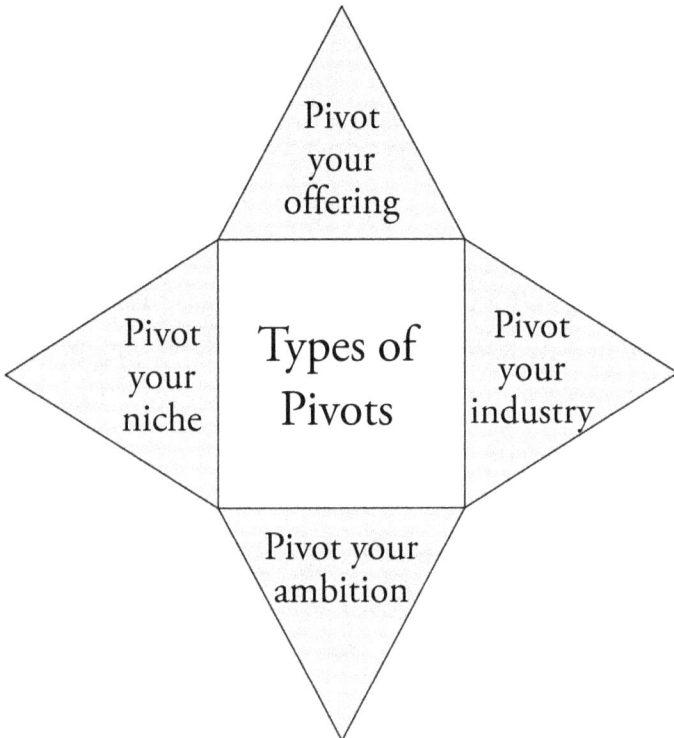

Pivot your offering

This is by far the most common approach to a pivot in a company, startup or a business. In this type of pivot, you change your product to better meet the market conditions. Or you change your service to better match the needs of your customer.

For example, you are in the business of making bespoke comfortable work shoes to order. However, due to coronavirus and social distancing efforts around the world, most people are working from home. So you decide to pivot your core offering. You pivot to making custom wool slippers that are extra comfy and cozy. You haven't changed your customer or industry. You are still selling shoes to the same customer. However, you pivoted your product to better suit changing needs.

Sometimes you might decide to Zoom-in and reduce the line of products you sell or reduce the number of features in your software product. So you decide to double down on what's in demand and cut out any products and features that are not profitable.

This concept of Zooming-in was first coined by Eric Ries, father of "The Lean Startup" movement.

Similarly, another way to do this sort of pivot is to Zoom-out, where you add new products or features to deal with the changing landscape.

Pivot your industry

In this sort of pivot, you change your industry. For example, you run digital marketing campaigns and own a small Digital Marketing agency. Your agency mostly runs campaigns online for small to medium businesses.

In a recession, ad budgets are first to be cut. And people no longer want to pay someone ongoing fees to manage their digital marketing campaigns.

However, you realize that even though people do not want to pay for digital marketing services, they still want to attract clients online. And you have all the necessary skills to train someone to sell online.

So you decide to become a coach and start training people, which leads you to realize that you are really good at educating people. You find other good coaches like yourself and launch a coaching and educational platform.

This way, you have completely pivoted your industry from a Digital Marketing Agency to an educational and coaching marketplace.

Pivot your customer/niche

Another way to pivot is to continue to make the same product but change the niche that you are selling to.

For example, scientists at the pharmaceutical company Pfizer discovered the powers of Viagra (sildenafil citrate) by accident in the early Nineties during trials of a potential new angina drug named UK-92480.

Angina is a condition in which the vessels that supply the heart with blood constrict, triggering chest pain and breathlessness.

UK-92480 was found to do little to relieve pain, and Pfizer was on the verge of abandoning the drug when reports began to show a distinctive pattern; many male trial volunteers were experiencing an unusual side-effect . . . erections.

Rather than dilating their coronary blood vessels as hoped, the blood vessels of their penises became dilated instead.

Senior Pfizer scientist Chris Wayman investigated what was happening by testing the drug on penile tissue samples from impotent men. The effect was dramatic.

Pfizer was clever enough to not let this lucky accident go to waste, and immediately pivoted this new drug as an Erectile Dysfunction remedy. This made

Pfizer billions of dollars in revenue for the coming years.

Many times companies pivot by simply changing their pricing strategy.

Pivot your ambition

You do not always have to just pivot your product, industry, or customer. In some cases, people change their vision or find their own purpose.

At some stage, Mark Zuckerberg had to realize that the Facemash ("hot or not" type website) or TheFacebook made just for Harvard students, could be made bigger. And that it could be used by billions of people around the world every day, and that he could do something about it.

I have seen this happen with individuals' careers and with multiple startups. It is either when people find a purpose for social good or realize what they are really passionate about.

For example, you are working with a fintech startup, and after a lucrative exit, you decide to fight climate change and go on a mission to make the human race a multi-planetary species. AKA - Elon Musk. Or after retiring from running an exceptional software giant, you decide to spend the rest of your life improving the average human life expectancy and saving 100's of millions of lives in the developing world. AKA - Bill Gates.

These are the types of pivots that I find most exciting. Because following your purpose and vision are always going to be more powerful than chasing revenue and EBITDA (Earnings Before Interest, Taxes, Depreciation, and Amortization).

In conclusion:

- *A pivot is a change in direction or tactics to reach your ultimate long term goal.*
- *A pivot at the right time can be extremely advantageous to your career, business, or startup.*
- *You can pivot your product or service by changing what you offer, who you offer it to, or the industry you operate in.*
- *The most powerful pivots happen when you find your purpose and vision.*

SHOULD YOU PERSIST INSTEAD OF PIVOTING?

Most businesses struggling during these disruptive times are posed with this question. Should they just continue instead of pivoting? Before we tackle that question, I would like to look a bit deeper into persisting.

To persist means to continue one's course of action despite difficulty or opposition. If you look at most business or personal success stories, you are more than likely to find stories of persistence against all odds.

According to Michael Siebel, the founder of Twitch:

"Good entrepreneurs, founders, and leaders get stuff done despite the odds. They have a consistent ability to say that they will do something, and then they do it. They do not get stuck in the execution stage. It doesn't mean they get everything right 100%, just that they do not get stuck in the execution stage.

They don't say that they want to do something and come back two weeks later and say that they couldn't do it. They always figure out a way to get some version of it done and learn from it."

This sort of ability to get stuff done despite the circumstances shows the persistent character of the founder.

As an example, let's look at the story of Brandon Stanton, the founder of Humans of New York.

Brandon Stanton demonstrated an extremely high level of persistence and grit.

He spent over six years taking thousands, if not tens of thousands of photographs of people from all walks of life and in different parts of the globe. If you know only this part of the story of Brandon, you could easily mistake his persistence for his love for photography. But Brandon displayed a high level of commitment to whatever he was doing. When he felt that he wasn't getting enough knowledge from his formal university education, he set a goal for himself.

His goal was to read 100 pages of non-fiction every day. He maintained this for years. Regardless of how boring or heavy a book might be, if he started it, he would read 100 pages that day.

Yes indeed, Brandon had a major pivot in his career from trading bonds to telling stories. But after that pivot, Brandon has stuck with his passion and calling for many years. He didn't give up after taking five or ten photographs and a few short blogs. He didn't just pivot a few months or a year into his photography career to become a consultant or Business Analyst. Nothing wrong with either of those professions, I just want to point out that Brandon showed steadfast persistence for over half a decade in following his dream and passion.

Luckily, Brandon knew when to Pivot and when to Persist. And we all get to enjoy Humans of New York. Brandon went on to raise US3.8 million dollars in 2016 for a pediatric cancer research center. He created a fundraising campaign from the photographs that he had taken in the Pediatrics Department of Memorial Sloan Kettering Cancer Center in New York City.

We can learn about his story, and hindsight might make it feel like it is an easy decision. However, having perseverance when times are tough is not easy.

Another name for the level of persistence that Brandon had displayed is GRIT.

According to the well-known Psychologist Dr. Angela Lee Duckworth

> *"Grit is passion and perseverance for very long-term goals. Grit is having stamina. Grit is sticking with your future, day-in, day-out. Not just for the week, not just for the month, but for years. And working really hard to make that future a reality. Grit is living life like it's a marathon, not a sprint."*

I believe that the ability to have GRIT is extremely important for any entrepreneur wanting to win.

As an author, I go to multiple events every year as a speaker. Most of the events I speak at are on the topics of entrepreneurship, startups, and innovation.

At these sorts of events and at my work, ProductDone.com, I meet large numbers of founders and entrepreneurs. Most of them lack the ability to focus on one task. They are highly entrepreneurial, so their brain continuously bombards them with new ideas. It often feels like they are in a room full of hundreds of jack-in-the-box toys opening spontaneously; each jack-in-the-box is popping up with a new opportunity that they should go after.

I know this feeling because I am an entrepreneur at heart, and I have struggled with focus in the past. I see opportunities everywhere. And I know that I have to persist and go after the one thing that I really, really want. In times like these, I am reminded of this quote.

"Be like a postage stamp. Stick to
one thing until you get there."
- Josh Billings

I sometimes observe a housefly, and it goes back and forth and sideways. Sometimes it keeps doing that without getting anywhere. Every time you get distracted in a side project and go sideways or back and forth, you are not covering the distance you could otherwise cover.

On the other end of the spectrum are the tiny Godwit birds that fly all the way from Alaska to New Zealand for their annual migration. Their journey is about 11,000km or 7,000 miles. They fly this non-stop as they cannot land on the sea. These tiny 400gm birds show the level of grit and focus that most humans cannot imagine. I find it inconvenient to even travel on long haul flights from New Zealand.

History books and autobiographies are full of great people who stuck to their guns despite over-whelming odds. They were formidable. Their characters overflowed with grit and unworldly persistence.

In the next chapter, I want to address the times in your personal or business life when you should persist instead of pivoting.

Conclusion

- It is not easy to have the wisdom to decide whether you should persist or pivot.
- Good entrepreneurs and founders persist and show grit when things get tough.
- Being formidable is a key trait of great founders and entrepreneurs.

REASONS NOT TO PIVOT

Most of this book is dedicated to pivoting in times of disruption. However, there are many occasions in life and business when you should persist. Jumping from one idea to another serves no one. Just because you have failed once or twice doesn't automatically mean you should completely pivot.

Success and failure sometimes go hand in hand. If you pick up any history book, you will come across stories of successful people that started as failure or faced failure multiple times in their career or business.

Failure is just part of life. As long as you learn from your failure and continue to implement those learnings next time, it is all good. Practicing this sort of behavior and not letting failure stop you from trying again makes you formidable.

When I think about being formidable, this quote comes to mind.

> *"I've missed more than 9000 shots in my career. I've lost almost 300 games. 26 times, I've been trusted to take the game winning shot and missed. I've failed over and over and over again in my life. And that is why I succeed."*
> *Michael Jordan*

If you stop persisting, then you won't fail; however, you will definitely not succeed or learn anything new. Failure is a great teacher that allows you an opportunity to improve. The quote above doesn't mention it, but from every missed shot, Michael Jordan improved his skills. Every lost game enabled him to think, what went wrong? What went badly? And strategize, what can I do differently next time? What do I need to practice? Losing games and clutch shots didn't make him pivot to another career.

Even the people and businesses who have pivoted in their lifetime, have still shown grit and persistence in their careers.

From my experience and observation, I believe that there are three times in life or business when you shouldn't pivot.

- People love your product.
- Your product is going to change humanity forever.
- It matters more than just financial success.

People love your product

I am currently CEO and Cofounder of ProductDone. At ProductDone, we help founders, entrepreneurs, and startups with bringing their idea to life. Every day I talk with 3 to 4 founders who have an idea and need help with bringing their tech idea to life.

The first thing I look at is the founder's existing connection to the problem they want to solve. Because that tells me about how well they understand the problem. In most cases, entrepreneurs just have an idea about a product. Instead of focusing on solving a problem, they focus on their product or service. This leads to people launching products and services that no one wants.

The second thing I look at is user engagement over user acquisition. User acquisition can be bought. You can use clever marketing, promotions, sales tactics, etc., to acquire a large number of users. However, user engagement cannot be bought. People keep using your product only if it is extremely useful, solves a problem, or is addictive. In my books, user engagement is the real test that you have achieved product-market fit.

Despite the change in the business environment, people still love your product or service and use it all the time. Then it is a good sign that you should not pivot. It is time for you to dig in and persevere.

Your product is going to change humanity forever

Maybe you are working on a goal so audacious that you are even afraid to tell people. Maybe it is something that might take generations to achieve; you are just laying the foundations. You are working on technologies that are still just confined to science fiction.

If you are able to achieve your ambitions, then it will completely change the course of human history. Your invention or the foundation that your business is laying will positively impact the future of the human race.

For example, the goal of your organization is to extend the human lifespan to 200 years. Or you can tackle environmental and climate change. Or you are researching bacteria that can process plastic and convert it into fertile soil.

The loftier your goal, the more setbacks you are likely to face initially. You are forever going to feel under-resourced and underfunded. And a changing economic climate will only make it harder. This is your opportunity to show grit and prove your mettle.

So if you are studying or working on a world-changing idea, then my recommendation is to keep going. Move the human race forward. Do it for the next generation.

It matters more than just financial success

There is a third scenario in which I believe that you should not pivot — if you are working on something that has a larger community good. For example, you are managing an orphanage in a developing country. Or you run a soup kitchen and rehabilitation center.

Economic disruption always puts a lot of pressure on such facilities. Times such as the GFC and the Great Depression always put huge amounts of stress on organizations working for social good, because that's when they are also needed the most.

There is this quote by the artist Banksy –

"If you get tired, learn to
rest, not to quit."

So if your life, career, business, or organization is bringing a larger positive change to the community, then keep going. Regardless of how hard things get. You might have to pivot your approach on how you run things or fundraise in times of disruption. But persist and keep moving towards achieving your larger mission.

Conclusion

- To Persist is to stick to your long term goals through thick and thin.
- Having Grit, Perseverance, and Focus is essential for the long term success of your startup, business, or career.
- It can be extremely hard to have the wisdom to know when to Persevere and when to Pivot.
- You should persist and not pivot if people love your product and continue to use it regardless of the changing business environ-

ment. You should also persist if your idea is going to change humanity forever, or finally, if it is for something that is more than just financial success.

CONTRARIAN APPROACH TO BUSINESS?

Most businesses continue doing what has worked. I am sure you have heard the proverb before, *"If it ain't broke, don't fix it."*

And I do not blame them for following this approach. When I ran an ecommerce business, and some of our efforts were bringing in money, then we would keep doing that.

As you saw in the previous two chapters, persisting rather than pivoting can have advantages. So do you even need to pivot? Why take this contrarian approach?

During your career, life, business, or startup, you will be faced with this question; should you persist or pivot? I see it like a fork in the road. Where you either keep doing what you and others have been doing, and what previous generations did, or you pivot and find a completely new way. You forge your own path.

In times like these, I am reminded of this poem by Robert Frost.

The Road Not Taken

Two roads diverged in a yellow wood,
And sorry I could not travel both
And be one traveler, long I stood
And looked down one as far as I could

To where it bent in the undergrowth;
Then took the other, as just as fair,
And having perhaps the better claim,
Because it was grassy and wanted wear;
Though as for that the passing there
Had worn them really about the same,

And both that morning equally lay
In leaves no step had trodden black.
Oh, I kept the first for another day!

Yet knowing how way leads on to way,
I doubted if I should ever come back.

I shall be telling this with a sigh
Somewhere ages and ages hence:
Two roads diverged in a wood, and I—
I took the one less traveled by,
And that has made all the difference.

- Robert Frost

Deciding which fork to take is really hard. Most people choose to keep doing what they have always done. That is the path they know and have already traveled on. The unknown path is scary.

Here are some examples of people who took the path less traveled.

Annoyed by late fees when renting DVDs, Marc Randolph and Reed Hastings set out on a mission to remove this friction from watching movies at home. In 1998 they launched a DVD rental business called Netflix.

A year later, they introduced a monthly subscription model. In this model, you would pay Netflix a subscription fee, and every month, Netflix would send DVDs to your home. There would be no late fees. You just get new DVDs once you return the old ones.

By 2007 Netflix had accumulated 10 million monthly customers. Their revenue had grown from 150 million in 2002 to 1.2 Billion by 2007. By February 2007, it had distributed its billionth DVD. That success and that kind of growth should have convinced any company to stick to what's working. For Netflix, it was apparent in the early 2000s that their core competency was in distribution and logistics.

At this point, most other businesses would keep to their current trajectory and keep persisting. However, Netflix chose to neglect the known path and decided to pivot towards a path less traveled.

When I look at the Netflix pivot, it was so radical and ambitious that few people could see it, let alone understand it, and the pivot/transitions weren't easy. At one point, Netlflix lost 800,000 subscribers. But it was a short term pain that Netflix was willing to take for long term gain.

Netflix could see the disruption that Youtube was bringing. They understood very well that, just as they had disrupted Blockbuster, a streaming service could disrupt their DVD rental service. So instead of letting someone else disrupt them, Netflix disrupted itself and pivoted into a streaming service, later on also becoming a content producing studio.

From 1998 to 2007, Netflix's revenue steadily grew year on year along with the number of monthly subscribers. Most businesses who experience similar revenue and share price growth do not even dream about pivoting. Netflix decided to do the contrary. Netflix pivoted again and became a major content producer and buyer globally.

Growth can hide systemic problems

I often exchange ideas about business, management, and startups with friends. One such friend, Kenneth Leong, has started multiple businesses and successfully exited some. He often says that "Growing revenue can hide a lot of problems."

I see this with so many startups and established businesses. They feel like they have a successful business, and then something happens, and they feel like the rug was pulled out from under their feet. Their industry or niche gets disrupted by a new player, change in regulation, or a recession. They think they could not have seen it coming.

Many entrepreneurs believe that you only need to pivot when you are consistently missing your KPIs.

However, pivoting should be a vital tool in any CEO's toolkit even when it seems like everything is going fine.

It is always better to pivot on your terms than be forced to pivot to revive your business, especially if you have run out of resources.

History is littered with companies that didn't pivot when they should have.

One such company is Kodak.

In the year 2005, Kodak had annual revenue of over US$11 Billion. Digital photography was still in its infancy during the early 2000s. But the writing was on the wall. Pivot now to stay relevant or be lost in the pages of business history books.

While Kodak did create and market the first digital cameras, it is important to note that it placed all of its faith in the analog film market throughout the 1970s, '80s, and '90s. Since the business was always massively profitable throughout its history, it seemed like a sure bet.

Kodak's leadership decided to keep walking on the path they had traveled for over 100 years.

Later on, Kodak tried to make the leap into the digital commercial market, but it was far too late to compete with companies like Sony and Canon that had already claimed their shares.

Technological disruption proved deadly to Kodak. Kodak filed for Chapter 11 bankruptcy protection in January 2012.

Make yourself redundant

The key concept to take home from this chapter is that even if things are going well, think about how you can make yourself redundant. Disrupt yourself before someone else does that for you.

In the early 2000s, I could foresee that digital marketing and ecommerce was going to disrupt offline retail. However, if you worked in retail, it would be hard to justify any investment into ecommerce when 99% of your revenue was still from offline channels.

When you think about disrupting your own business in good times, you end up finding ways to make your business bulletproof in times of downturn.

For example, you own a well-known chain of restaurants that sell fried chicken. Business is good; sales are on a steady growth, and expenses are stable.

So you should start thinking about what can disrupt your business. Firstly think about hypothetical scenarios that can disrupt your business.

Scenario 1: The main ingredient you use gets disrupted, there is a bird flu or some other calamity, and you are unable to source chickens. So you start testing vegan meats made from legumes or soy.

Scenario 2: HR costs go out of proportion. So you start automating as much as possible.

Scenario 3: Behavioral changes — people start enjoying cooking instead of eating out. So you start selling ready-to-make kits. These kits have all the instructions and ingredients to make fried chicken, similar to your restaurant, at home.

Scenario 4: People prefer using an app to order instead of calling and ordering take away. So you start investigating alternative methods of paying and ordering from your restaurants.

The ideal time to implement things like these is when times are good because you have more resources to devote to trying and developing solutions.

In the next chapter, we will look at some companies that successfully pivoted at the right time, leading to exponential growth.

Conclusion

Technology will keep moving at an ever-faster pace. You will need to find new ways of doing things that are more efficient and more effective. That might mean pivoting and taking the path less traveled.

If we lived in a static world where nothing ever changed — fashion never changed, languages never changed, laws never changed, technology and social norms never changed — then you could just do what has always worked in the past. However, we live in an ever-changing world, where everything is in a constant state of flux. We need to constantly adapt to the ever-changing world, so we do not end up like dinosaurs such as Blockbuster and Kodak.

Pivot yourself before external disruption forces you to, by that time it could be too late.

SUCCESSFUL STARTUP PIVOTS

Unlike Kodak and Blockbuster, here are three stories of successful startups that pivoted at the right time.

Their pivots helped them achieve a product-market fit and established their tech startups as market leaders in their respective categories.

1: Burbn

During his school days, Kevin was obsessed with becoming a DJ. At one point, he pestered a vinyl-record shop to give him a part-time job. This stint working part-time at the vinyl shop led to him getting gigs to open for other DJs.

There was just one problem; he wasn't even 18 yet, no one trusted or believed in him. For Kevin, what he lacked in age, he made up for in determination and focus for whatever task he was working on.

When he finished Collthe University, Kevin got employed by the famous internet service and technology giant 'Google' as an associate product marketing manager. His duties at Google entailed working on Gmail, Google Calendar, Docs, Spreadsheets, and other products.

Kevin left Google after working there for two years. He went ahead to form a new venture called "Nextstop" alongside other ex-Googlers. While working at Nextstop, he came up with the idea of developing the next big thing in the world of the internet

His experience working at Nextstop helped Kevin improve his coding skills, and he started working on the idea of a location-based app with inspiration from Foursquare.

Kevin, being a fan of Kentucky Whiskeys, named this app "Burbn." Burbn was a web app that allowed its users to check into locations, make plans, earn points from hanging out with friends, post pictures, and lots more. He managed to raise a seed round of US$500,000 with Baseline Ventures and Andreessen Horowitz.

Burbn was not, however, terribly successful, although the seed funding helped Kevin bring in Mike Krieger. Together they paid attention to how the people were using it. And they were unsatisfied with the amount of traction and user engagement they were getting with Burbn.

At this point, they had to make a choice whether to continue and persist with Burbn as it is or Pivot.

The Burbn Pivot

Kevin and Mike realized that Burbn was too complicated; it was a jumble of features that made it confusing. They used analytics to determine how exactly their customers were using Burbn.

Their findings?

People weren't using Burbn's check-in features at all. Burbn's users were mainly using the app's photo-sharing features. They were posting and sharing photos like crazy.

At that point, Kevin and Mike decided to double down on their data and findings: They focused on their photo-sharing infrastructure and scrapped almost everything else. Burbn would Pivot to become a simple photo-sharing app.

In the book ZigZag: The Surprising Path to Creativity, Keith Sawyer says:

"They began by studying all of the popular photography apps, and they quickly homed in on two main competitors. Hipstamatic was cool and had great filters, but it was hard to share your photos. Facebook was the king of social networking, but its iPhone app didn't have a great photo-sharing feature. Mike and Kevin saw an opportunity to slip in between Hipstamatic and Facebook by developing an easy-to-use app that made social photo-sharing simple. They chopped everything out of Burbn except the photo, comment, and like features."

They also added filters. But simplicity remained their focus. In their final version, you could post a photo in three clicks.

After months of experimentation and prototyping—on October 12, 2010—Systrom and Krieger released a simple photo-sharing app. It was named not Burbn, but Instagram.

The rest is history…

2: Tune in, Hook up

"They offered single women on Craigslist $20 to upload videos of themselves"

- This is the story of the failed start and Pivot of an extremely successful platform.

After Paypal, Chad Hurley, Steve Chen, and Javed Karim wanted to co-found a company that had something to do with video. They could see that video was the new big thing. They thought that the obvious application for video would be dating.

"We always thought there was something with video there, but what would be the actual practical application?" Chen said at the South by Southwest tech, film and music conference in Austin, Texas,2006. "We thought dating would be the obvious choice."

Despite bringing people to use their website, no one came forward and uploaded videos. Even 14 years later, most of the popular dating websites have photographs and UX at the center of their strategy and not video.

Tune in, Hook ups, Pivot

Chad, Steve, and Javed, pivoted from being a dating app and decided to open it up to all videos. They decided to call it YouTube. Javed uploaded the first video of his trip to Zoo. His 18-second video might seem insignificant. However, it was the first video on the world's most popular video streaming platform, Youtube, getting over 85 million views.

After a Beta testing period, the site launched in December 2005, and a Nike commercial became the first video to receive one million views.

YouTube continued to garner exponential growth and funding. In October 2009, Google announced that it would acquire Youtube for a cool US$1.65 Billion.

After their successful pivot and merging into Google, YouTube went from strength to strength. It is estimated that in 2007, YouTube consumed as much bandwidth as the entire Internet in 2000. Now in 2020, hundreds of billions of hours of videos have been watched on YouTube during its existence. And Youtube has become a tech juggernaut that impacts culture globally.

3: Tote

Like so many new ventures, it all started with brainstorming. Ben Silbermann and Paul Sciarra started bouncing ideas around what you can do on a phone that would be different from doing the same thing on a PC.

You have to remember that this is 2008-'09, the iPhone was still just a baby, less than two years old. Most of the internet, web, and software was made for desktop computing.

They started thinking, "What are the things we could do on the phone that would be different than what we can do on the computer?"

First concept: Make a social trivia game.

In this trivia game, anyone can write trivia on any topic, and anyone on the planet can play.

Ben and Paul wanted to make something that is useful to lots of people around the world.

Second concept: Make a digital catalog system.

Paul and Ben noticed that so many people were getting catalogs delivered to their house. They felt that the mail order catalog system was completely archaic and ripe for disruption. If this were made into an app, it would save so much paper, and people would be able to search for what they wanted.

This idea became the foundation of Tote.

As soon as they had decided what they were going to build, they went forth and started raising capital. The efforts to raise capital didn't go as planned.

However, Ben Silbermann was extremely persistent; he didn't just pivot his idea immediately again. When they failed to raise money, he started looking for business competitions to win so he could get some seed capital to get this idea built. Ben Silbermann, Paul Sciarra, and Vikram Bhaskara's idea didn't win the first prize, but they won the audience choice awards at the NYU Stern's Berkley Center for Entrepreneurship & Innovation 10th Annual Business Plan Competition. This led them to an introduction to Brian Cohen, who became their first investor.

After the trio had secured the initial backing of an Angel Investor, they wanted to design Tote to change shopping on a mobile phone. The goal was to take it from being a pain to easy and fun.

According to its Facebook site, Tote connected consumers with dozens of retailers, including Banana Republic, jCrew, Nordstrom, American Apparel, etc. They launched this app in 2009. Tote's app would let customers save their favorite items, alerted them about sales, and helped with finding nearby stores.

Tote's main objective was to make shopping through your iPhone fun and easy. Tote wanted to disrupt clothing and online retail.

So what happened.

While Tote was a suitable replacement for physical catalogs that mostly ended up in the recycling bin. Tote was lacking a crucial component to make online retail seamless. At the time of Tote's release, the payment technology just wasn't advanced enough to allow for simple, on-the-go transactions. The lack of a workable transaction system was more than a little inconvenient for an app that marketed itself as making shopping more convenient. It threatened its very existence.

But while users of Tote weren't using it to buy items, they were saving their selections and growing their lists of saved "favorites" items. According to a quote from Ben Silbermann in a FastCompany article, "I used to collect insects as a kid, this was yet another example of people's tendency to share their collections with one another."

Tote's pivot

After launching Tote, Silbermann pivoted to offer people a visually appealing way to display all their collections—whether they were books, adorable dog images, or women's clothes—on the same site.

When their investors heard of the plan of Ben Silbermann, they doubled down on their investment, and Pinterest was born.

WHEN A COUNTRY PIVOTS

"Every Challenge is an
opportunity for growth"
- Sam Kamani

ivots are not limited to just startups. Economic
and technological change is unstoppable.
Individuals, corporates, organizations, and governments all have to pivot at times and adapt to changing environments.

As I have spent most of the last 20 years in New
Zealand, I am aware of the times when things got
really tough for New Zealand economically. New

Zealand had to collectively decide if she was going to continue flogging a dead horse or if she was going to innovate and pivot.

Luckily New Zealand has been blessed with extraordinary leaders. That's why, despite being a small isolated island nation at the end of the world, New Zealand has still managed to thrive and prosper.

In the 1930s and '40s, Britain took nearly 90% of all goods exported from New Zealand. New Zealand had all its eggs in just one basket. If anything were to happen to Britain's economy, it would severely affect New Zealand farmers.

That is precisely what happened in the early 1970s. The United Kingdom joined the European Communities on 1 January 1973, along with Denmark and the Republic of Ireland. The EC would later become the European Union. European Economic Community nations had agreed on a 'common agricultural policy,' which effectively excluded outside producers from the European market. They justified this by arguing the need to secure food supply in the event of war or other disruption, and to sustain rural communities.

This meant an end to New Zealand being able to export agricultural products to Britain.

When you are unable to sell to your largest customer, then suddenly, you are in trouble. It could happen to an individual or a company or even a country.

So how did New Zealand respond?

From the early 1960s to 1973, New Zealand fought against the trade policy. However, that had only limited success and bought New Zealand time to prepare for its pivot.

New Zealand realized that just like the EU, it would have to form its own partnerships with nation states to allow free flow of trade. Ten years later, New Zealand signed its first free trade agreement. The Closer Economic Relations (CER) Agreement between New Zealand and Australia came into effect in 1983.

This pivot set New Zealand on the bold path to accomplish similar free trade agreements with other countries around the pacific.

In 2008 New Zealand became the first developed country to sign a free trade agreement with China.

From the 1980s onwards, New Zealand exports continued to grow. Now China and Australia are the two largest export and import trading partners for New Zealand.

Being pushed away from Britain was initially very hard for New Zealand. However, it enabled New Zealand and its people to better equip for the next century. In the early 1970s, the United Kingdom's GDP was more than China's GDP. Today in 2020, the size of the Chinese economy is many times bigger than the UK's economy.

This wasn't the only time New Zealand had to pivot.

At its peak, there were over 70 million sheep in New Zealand, and New Zealand relied heavily on wool, carpet, and lamb exports.

At the end of 1966, the price of wool was cut by 40% as it was replaced by a synthetic fiber. This posed a large issue for New Zealand as wool was one of its top exports. The entire economy underwent a diversification period to recover.

New Zealand began looking for an alternative source of capital via exporting goods as it was no longer able to trade with Britain. The loss of wool in 1966 and the depression of meat prices meant that change had to happen fast if the economy was to still operate at a functioning level. Until the 1960s, New Zealand had operated primarily by exporting pastoral products such as butter, meat, and wool.

New Zealand pivoted again

New Zealand lessened its reliance on sheep and wool. The number of sheep in New Zealand has come down from 70 million in the 1960s and '70s to 27.4 million in 2019.

New Zealand has also pivoted away from reliance just on farming and diversified into tourism, wine, pharmaceuticals, and technology.

By 2008 the single biggest export good was tourism, bringing in over a quarter of the total export revenue.

Sometimes when you are forced, because of regulation change or technological change, to pivot, then it can be a positive development in the long term for your company, career, or economy. You may discover opportunities that you never dreamed of.

"Change is the only Constant"
- Heraclitus

New Zealand is not the only country to face disruption. Every country or group of people around the world are going to face disruption at some point in their life cycle.

Dubai's story

Dubai's economy was built on the back of the oil industry, which developed rapidly after oil was first struck in the mid-1960s. But Dubai's oil reserves paled in comparison to its neighboring cities and states. It is estimated that Dubai's neighboring emirate Abu Dhabi has nearly 20 times more oil reserves than Dubai.

From the early days, Dubai has known that it is going to run out of oil reserves, and it needs to pivot its economy away from oil.

Dubai diversified by building the world's largest man-made harbor and biggest port in the Middle East, Jebel Ali. Also, Dubai built a large number of hotels, entertainment venues, and a massive airport in order to position itself as a regional hub for travel and tourism.

Today oil makes up less than 5% of Dubai's economy. Dubai continues to diversify and invest in new technologies and niches. For example, Dubai is in the process of building one of the world's largest solar power plants and has indicated a high level of interest in investing in Artificial Intelligence and automation.

Conclusion

This economic disruption could be a blessing in disguise. Regardless of whether you are a person, company, state, or a country, if you embrace this opportunity to pivot and find new niches, then, in the long run, you will end up in a much better situation than you were before.

PIVOTING YOUR CAREER

There is no one magic answer to this question. Pivoting and changing your career is not something you do instantly or as a result of a knee jerk reaction.

Most career pivots happen over time. As people navigate their way through their education, jobs, businesses, and life, they forge a unique pathway for their own careers.

My pivots

When I look at my own career journey, I have pivoted quite a few times in my career, sometimes knowingly and sometimes coincidentally.

After completing my Bachelors in Computer Application in India, I moved to New Zealand as an international student to study marketing. That was my first pivot, moving from computer science to marketing. This was intentional.

I grew up in a family where my parents were excellent artists but lacked the skills to market and sell effectively. Growing up, our house was full of artwork that no one ever purchased. That's why I have understood the importance of sales and marketing from a very young age. That was my motivation for changing from computer science to marketing.

After graduating from a university in New Zealand as an international student, I was starting my career with a huge student loan and very limited job prospects. I had to do all sorts of jobs to survive, from working on farms for minimum wage to clipping tickets at a ferry terminal for two years.

While I was doing odd jobs for minimum pay, I kept updating myself. In the early 2000s, the internet wasn't the beast it is today. So I used to spend my evenings and weekends at the library or Borders book shop.

Having a background in software development and technology, I knew the potential software had to disrupt the world. Also, having studied marketing, I knew the importance of customer acquisition for any business.

In 2004 I had one of those light bulb moments where I realized that the internet and software would completely disrupt marketing, retail, and customer acquisition. It hardly seems like an insight now. In 2004 people laughed at me when I shared my future predictions with them. In 2004 Youtube didn't exist, and TheFaceBook only existed for Harvard students.

The total ecommerce spend in 2004 for the USA was only 1.6%, the remaining 98.4% was still through brick and mortar stores and other traditional retail channels.

I don't blame anyone for not listening to me back then. Most businesses are going to worry about their 98.4% of business instead of going after 1.6%

So I started learning as much as I could about digital marketing. I also started connecting with business people and advising them about acquiring customers online. This provided me with an opportunity to join a small company in the nutritional supplement niche to help them transition to ecommerce from phone and catalog sales. I delivered exponential growth to that company and ended up becoming Managing Director and a shareholder.

I sold that business after running it for seven years. Part of my motivation to exit from that business was to go back into tech. I still wanted to do marketing in one way or another but for a product that is more scalable. Physical products, especially if they are in the pharmaceutical space, are a lot harder to scale compared to most software products.

This time my pivot was a lot more drastic. I went from selling supplements online to working for an esports company, where we made software to run Esports tournaments, and we built a platform that was like Air Miles for Gaming—Uproar.gg

Once again, I helped this esports startup with customer acquisition and grew from 60,000 monthly active users to 300,000 monthly active users in eight months. This startup was acquired in 2018.

After the esports startup, I started an agency to help other entrepreneurs develop MVPs from their ideas. I am still running this company—ProductDone. com.

While I am managing and running ProductDone, I like to dabble in side projects. That is why in March 2020, I assembled a team to work together on a startup.

In this startup, I intend to combine my experience of working in the esports industry and my trading knowledge to build a platform that gamifies trading and investing. You can find out more about it at Ensydr.com.

Because of my journey and pivots from working on farms and clipping tickets to managing businesses, two exits, and building startups, I decided to share what I do.

So I started speaking at events, mentoring entrepreneurs, and jumped into writing books.

I co-authored "The 30 Day Startup" in early 2019, and that book is bought by thousands of people around the world every month.

Some of my pivots were intentional, like going from coding to marketing. This has given me unique technical knowledge that many other marketers lack. However, some of my pivots have been purely incidental, for example, writing a book and then enjoying the process so much that I kept writing, and public speaking.

There is no set formula for what path your career should take. Pivots in your career will give you a unique combination of experience and skills that might help you in the future. Most people do not know how their industry is going to be disrupted.

One thing is for certain, and that is your field of work is going to be disrupted in your lifetime. The pace of technological and societal change keeps on increasing. If it weren't coronavirus, then it would be something else.

We must always remain open to adapting to change.

Before you dig deeper into the practical ways that you can pivot, I would like to address two pieces of bad advice or thinking that doesn't work.

- What not to do -

Follow your passion

I am sure you have heard this before. DO NOT FOLLOW THIS ADVICE. Most people who give this advice have made it following their passion; however, they were lucky that their skill set and abilities intersected with their passion.

For example, if Michael Jordan said, follow your passion. You heard this advice, and you also love basketball; however, you are a 46-year-old female in Cambodia. Even if you follow your passion, it would be hard for you to play for the WNBA.

I have an alternative for this later in this chapter.

Already invested too much

"I should not pivot because I already spent four years studying something," or "I already have X number of years experience, I cannot waste this experience." I am sure you have heard all these things before.

There is a name for this—"SUNK CAUSE FALLACY"—where you are in a career or business, and you are no good at it, and you dislike it with passion. Don't let your decisions be tainted by the emotional investments you accumulate.

Consider it as a sunk cost and move on. The faster you make the decision, and the faster you move, the better you would be.

WHAT you should do instead

- Skill + Interest

Look for the cross-section of skill and interest. Ask yourself, what are you good at? And what are you interested in? I believe that it is much better to ask these two questions than ask yourself what you are passionate about.

- What are you currently doing

Most of the innovation happens at the edges or the cross-section of two fields. You are really good at maths and interested in behavioral psychology, so, maybe you could write a mathematical algorithm explaining the movements or purchasing habits of people. Examine the field you are currently working in, and then ask yourself, where else or which other fields can my knowledge be applied to?

- What problems can you solve

I firmly believe that most startups should be focused on solving real problems. The bigger the problem you solve, the bigger the reward. The same applies to individual careers. What problems can you solve? And who can you solve them for? Start connecting with those people.

For example, when I started writing this book, I asked myself — What problems can it solve? Who can it help?

My answer was — It can help entrepreneurs, startups, small to medium-size businesses, and fresh graduates. They are finding it challenging because of all the disruption. They want to learn about how to pivot their career or company. My book will help them learn everything they need to know about how to pivot, adapt, and overcome. And as the next step of this process, I started connecting with my target audience to get feedback.

- Look at making yourself obsolete

Every now and then, I give myself this thinking exercise — How can I make myself obsolete? I did that even in the nutraceutical business I owned. My idea was to work **on** the business and not **in** the business. It is very easy to just get busy and stop working on the business. Making yourself obsolete gives you enough time to reinvent yourself.

If you are not a business owner, then see if there is any tech that can make you obsolete in the next few years. Go and start learning about it and how people will implement it. Every new technology that is implemented creates a lot more indirect jobs compared to the direct jobs it replaces.

- It is a journey, not a destination

Any pivot takes time. Success in most people's career is a result of sustained effort. Keep making small efforts, keep learning, keep improving. Take small steps in the right direction.

I think this quote from one of my favorite authors sums it up.

> *"Every action you take is a vote*
> *for the type of person you wish*
> *to become. No single instance*

will transform your beliefs, but
as the votes build up, so does the
evidence of your new identity."
— **James Clear,**

Realize that it is just something that will take time
- Start by finding a side gig, volunteering, build something with friends.

You do not have to completely leave your current job or education and pivot 100%. You can dip your toes first to check if it is something for you.

As mentioned previously in the book, I am currently working on a startup where we are gamifying finance. The team that I have assembled are all working on it part-time, including myself. We are doing it for the process and not the final product. Our first goal is to provide an engaging experience for our users. Until we achieve that goal, all of us will keep working on it part-time.

Find a side project or volunteer in the industry you want to work. If you cannot find anything suitable to join, then get together with your friends and start something yourself. You do not have to give up your full-time job initially.

- Upskill and reskill for minimal expense

It has never been easier to learn a new skill online for minimal expense. I still frequent YouTube, Udemy, Udacity, and many other online learning platforms to upskill myself in my spare time.

I might not use most of the new things I have learned; however, it still keeps me sharp. Also, you never know where you might use that skill.

Conclusion

Technology, politics, economy, and natural disasters will continue to bring change and disruption to every career or profession.

If your career is disrupted or you think it will be disrupted, then do the following to pivot your career.

- Find something at the cross-section of your skillset and interests.
- Look for something in an industry that is adjacent to yours.
- What problems can you solve?
- Make yourself obsolete.
- Find a side gig or volunteer to try new things.
- Upskill and learn new skills online.

PIVOTING YOUR LIFE

Most people pivot their careers slowly, or their expertise evolves over time. However, there are some people who completely overhaul their life. They do a complete U-turn.

Here is an example of a remarkable young man who did exactly that.

Brandon's venture has over 25 million followers on social media, has raised millions of dollars for people in need, brought strangers together, and has been recognized by Time magazine as "30 under 30." And he did all this, one photograph at a time.

Brandon didn't start his career as a photographer; he had a major pivot in his life. He changed from trading bonds to becoming Brandon Stanton, the world-renowned photographer who started the Humans of New York series. Brandon interviews people and publishes quotes and stories along with their photographs. The beauty of Humans of New York is not only the high-quality images or the composition or colors of photographs (even though they are great); the real reason for his success, in my view, is how Brandon gets people to open up to him and share their lives. These stories, in return, help the reader connect with Brandon's work at a much deeper level.

This is the story of Brandon's pivot. As a young man, he was a bonds trader. He planned to work in finance for a while so he could save and follow an artistic path later in life. But he found his job as a bonds trader stifling with no outlet for his creativity. As a means to exercise his creativity, Brandon purchased a camera and started photographing people in downtown Chicago on the weekends. Shortly after Brandon lost his job in the financial industry (during the Global Financial Crisis of 2007–2008), he decided to move to New York and photograph 10,000 people and tell their stories to the world.

Brandon's life and career had a major pivot. From trading and finance to capturing heartfelt stories of strangers and becoming a New York Times bestseller.

In Brandon's case, the job loss thrust him towards a pivot. However, it is not that clear in most cases.

A Pivot is nothing more than a change in direction.

In this case, Brandon pivoted his life instead of his business or product. However, a Pivot is a Pivot; you still have to conquer the doubt and uncertainty when making these sorts of decisions.

I have always been a fan of Humans of New York. However, I never knew about Brandon's personal story. One day while scrolling through some old podcasts of Tim Ferris, I saw the interview with Brandon Stanton. I would highly recommend that you listen to this podcast, interviewing Brandon about the big pivot in his personal career and life. Brandon is describing the challenges he faced just after his pivot from finance to photography.

Brandon went to New York and started photographing strangers. He would walk up to strangers and ask them if he could photograph them. People in New York are extremely busy; they do not have time for random strangers. Often he would have a string of rejections one after another; some rejections on the streets of New York aren't always polite.

Brandon found that the hardest part was when he had just gotten started. No one had heard of Humans of New York. None of his family or friends believed in his idea; some even thought he was crazy. He was continuously getting rejected by strangers; he started feeling insecure. This went on for months and it started to take a toll on him psychologically. He even started to doubt himself and his choice of pivoting his life.

When you pivot your life, it is abrupt and drastic. For example, you change your city, job, career, friends, etc.., everything at the same time. In Brandon's case, he had already lost his job in finance; on top of that, he completely changed his profession to be a photographer. He moved to another city; he didn't know many people in New York, so he had to make new friends.

At one point in Tim Ferriss' podcast, he asks Brandon, "What was the hardest part of all the challenges that you faced?" To which Brandon replied:

"It was all of the doubt, and not having any money, and nobody's paying attention, and I'm just doing this all day long for months, and all the tough shit was – and the loneliness too. I didn't know anybody in New York. I knew two people. And there was a Christmas break where those two people went home, and for two weeks, I

didn't see anybody that I knew. And I remember I spent Christmas Eve alone at a diner."

If you pivot your career, it is not going to be easy. You will go through the ups and downs. You might even have to battle self-doubt and ridicule from others. Especially in the early stages of your career when you still haven't got any success. The number of people who have completely pivoted their life is endless.

Sometimes people continue to reinvent themselves even at later stages in life. Do not let your past hold your dreams back.

Here are a few more examples of people who reinvented themselves at different stages of life.

Jeff Bezos had a lucrative career in computer science on Wall Street and took on top roles at various financial firms before transitioning to the world of ecommerce and launching Amazon when he was 31.

Dwayne "The Rock" Johnson pivoted his career not once, but twice. Before he was the muscle man who is in every single movie from 2018 - 2020, he was briefly a backup linebacker for the Canadian Football League's Calgary Stampeders. He ditched the football career and joined the World Wrestling Federation (WWF) in 1996 at 24, which catapulted him to stardom and allowed him to cross over to TV and movies in the early 2000s.

Arnold Schwarzenegger has made two major career pivots; he started out as an Austrian bodybuilder. He managed to win the world championship of bodybuilding multiple times in his 20s. In his 30s, he transitioned to become an A-list movie star, starring in many big-budget Hollywood movies. Then at the age of 56, he transitioned to politics and became the Governor of California.

Ray Kroc spent his career as a milkshake-device salesman before buying McDonald's at age 52 in 1954. He grew it into the world's biggest fast-food franchise.

If you have the right opportunity, then don't let age stop you from pivoting your career.

Conclusion

Pivoting your whole life is one of the hardest things you can imagine. Because not only are you changing your profession, in many cases you might also change your city, friends, daily routine, and more. This sort of drastic change can take you to some dark places mentally. However, if you are successful, then you end up creating a life that is beautiful, purposeful, and fulfilling. Scores of successful people have pivoted their life completely, and they haven't let things like location and age get in their way.

PIVOTING YOUR STARTUP OR BUSINESS

I am currently CEO and Cofounder of software development agency ProductDone. Apart from ProductDone, in my spare time, I work with another team on a startup called Ensydr.com

At Ensydr, we have decided that until we have a certain number of active users and a high level of engagement, we will bootstrap and self-fund it.

We will seek funding only when we are certain of our product-market fit. Product-market fit is the degree to which a product satisfies a strong market demand. I believe that product-market fit is crucial in building a successful and sustainable startup or business.

Ensydr.com will be a platform that gamifies trading and investment. Think of it like fantasy football; it will be like fantasy finance. For Ensydr.com, we will start by building an MVP. We will keep refining this MVP until it becomes something that people love to use. We want to make our product something people keep using and enjoy. So we will keep pivoting and experimenting with it until we get there.

How to pivot - Step by Step

Willingness to pivot

You have to be willing to pivot. So many times, I see startups and businesses that are married to their idea, product or service. Instead of finding a real product-market fit they would rather spend highly on Google and FB ads to try to get more users. That is because they love their initial idea or product so much, that instead of pivoting and making something that other people also love, they would rather make a loss.

I shared my journey of building the Ensydr platform because I want to inspire people to be open to change. It is hard to pivot right when you are mentally resistant to change.

Your goal should be to build or provide what your customers want.

Assets and strengths

Secondly, look at your current strengths and assets. When you are going through tough times, it is very easy to just focus on the negatives. Every startup or business has at least some strengths and assets. It might be your team, your people, your suppliers, your partners, your customers, your brand or your physical assets, etc.

Once you have stock of all your assets and strengths, then you know what you should be focusing on and what resources you will have to pivot.

Whenever there is a recession, depression, or a downturn, people focus on the essentials. The demand for "good to have" type products and services is generally a lot lower during a recession.

Many years ago, I read an article online that emphasized "be a painkiller, not a supplement." Figure out if your product or service is a supplement or a painkiller.

If your product or service is a supplement, then can you use your current assets and strengths to pivot and become a painkiller.

Stockdale Paradox

Follow the Stockdale paradox. The Stockdale Paradox is a concept that was popularized by Jim Collins in his book Good to Great.

It was named after James Stockdale, former vice presidential candidate, naval officer, and Vietnam prisoner of war.

Stockdale explained this idea as the following: "You must never confuse faith that you will prevail in the end — which you can never afford to lose — with the discipline to confront the most brutal facts of your current reality, whatever they might be."

In the most simplest explanation of this paradox, it's the idea of hoping for the best, but acknowledging and preparing for the worst.

Work out what the best-case scenario for your business is and work towards it. However, have a plan B for the worst-case scenario. Businesses who followed this principle, fared much better during the recession.

Move fast

Moving fast in disrupted times is essential. It is a massive advantage that early-stage startups and small businesses have over large corporations and enterprises. People in corporates, enterprise and government organizations have multiple layers of bureaucracy and internal politics to navigate. All that takes immense amounts of energy and introduces inefficiencies; it also takes time.

On the other hand, a small startup can find an uncrowded niche and build a solution ten times faster than a corporate, which will require the approval of five different committees, the board of directors, at least 18 zoom meetings, and 200 email threads.

As mentioned at the start of this book, I wanted to write a book on the value of Pivoting or Persisting in business. Due to the coronavirus pandemic, the world of business changed forever. I decided to pivot my book and pivot fast by taking action immediately. As soon as I decided to pivot, I started converting all the existing content I had written to suit the new economic environment. I started writing and writing and writing. I wrote most of this book in three weeks. Yes, it was nearly a month of late nights and weekends. But I moved fast. I did not have to navigate complex systems. I didn't have to get this idea passed through a board of directors; I didn't need approval from the overloads. I didn't have to get the blessings of Darth Vader, just my wife. I could just pivot and write something that would genuinely help people in this time.

I could move fast and pivot fast.

If you do not move fast, someone else in your industry will move fast and eat your cheese.

Be transparent, as soon as you have a decision

If you have a team, employees or subordinates then involve them. Be transparent with them in this process.

If they work directly with the customers, they might know and understand your customer much better. They might have suggestions that you have not thought about.

Be transparent with your customers if you need to pivot. Think of them as your extended network. They might be able to introduce you to someone valuable or even provide ideas and suggestions to make your startup or business better.

Start testing

By this point, you are willing to pivot immediately and have a good idea of your assets and strengths. You know what resources you can apply towards a pivot, and you have been transparent and open to getting feedback from clients, customers and business partners. You are expecting the best but prepared for the worst.

So in this phase, you will start testing your assumptions. Start in some small ways, build an MVP fast if it is a tech startup. In many cases, you do not even need to build the full MVP; you just make a demo of what your new product or service can do to gauge interest from prospective clients.

You know that you are pivoting in the right direction only if you are testing. If the idea of the new direction is a secret and just in your mind, then you don't know if your pivot will be successful or not.

Iterate

The goal of making an MVP is to learn from it and iterate. If you are not iterating, then you are not learning enough about your customer and the problem you intend to solve.

For example:

- If the sales cycle for your startup's product is too long, then something may need to change - people, process and/or product. Analyze all aspects of the sales discussion. Work with your marketing and sales team to work out how that can be improved. Iterate your pricing, quantities, warranties, etc. Iterate - test, iterate - test, iterate - test...

Make sure you are iterating all the time to ensure your product is in demand and relevant.

Train your brain to look for opportunities

It is easier to know what solution you should pivot to when you are able to spot opportunities. One way to enable yourself to spot opportunities is by being in the right frame of mind.

If you are always spending time with negative people, then you are more likely to think negatively and feel down. How much time do you spend with people who build you up and are always looking on the bright side of life?

It can be excruciatingly difficult to deal with negative people — people who bring your mood down with their pessimism, anxiety, and general sense of distrust. Imagine being constantly discouraged from pursuing your dreams because "very few people make it big." Constant exposure to negativity can make deep inroads into your bank of positivity, leading you to either become negative, diffident, anxious, or distrustful yourself.

If you want to be able to spot opportunities, then keep tabs on what you consume (read, listen, watch). If you are watching, reading, listening about other positive stories, then you are more likely to see that positivity around you and find new opportunities.

Your brain is just like your body. If you feed it a junk food diet, then it turns to garbage.

Are you feeding your brain a diet of gossip, rumors, conspiracy theories, and negative social media and politics?

Or

Are you providing your brain with a diet of meditation, gratitude, stories of positive people, creativity, art, stories about innovation, and tales of overcoming insurmountable odds?

Conclusion

In conclusion, make it your goal to delight your customers. If your product or service no longer does that, then it is time to relook at your offering.

To pivot your startup or business:

- Be willing to pivot.
- Look at your assets and strengths.
- Hope for the best, but prepare for the worst.
- Act on it fast.
- Communicate effectively and be transparent with your decision.
- Test - Iterate - Test.
- Spend time with positive people and train yourself to spot opportunities.

PIVOTING WITH NO MONEY

have no money, how can I pivot? Most of the time you can pivot without much money.

But before I get into that I would like to tell you the story of an entrepreneur who asked me for advice recently.

Entrepreneur: How do I find a cofounder?

Me: There are a few different ways; you can go to online marketplace-type websites like CoFoundersLab. You can go to hackathons, meetups, Startup Weekend, connect with people on Discord, Facebook groups, and Linkedin etc.

Entrepreneur: I am an introvert and I only talk with two or three people every event, I feel that is not enough.

Me: Why do you need a cofounder?

Entrepreneur: I have an idea for a tech startup, but I don't know how to build it, so I want someone who can code really well, to build it for me.

Me: Are you putting in your money into this startup or have you already raised funds?

Entrepreneur: No, I don't have any money to put in.

Me: Have you built startups before?

Entrepreneur: No, I am completely new to all this.

Me: What will your contribution to this startup be?

Entrepreneur: I will provide the idea.

Me: I think I know why you might be finding it hard to get a cofounder.

Then I explained to him that what you have right now is just the idea. Ideas just by themselves are worthless. Anyone can come up with ideas; you can come up with an idea in five mins, but implementation can take five months, five years, or even 50 years.

It is like building a house, you contact a construction company, and ask them to build the house with you. The construction company asks you what you will pay for the materials and labor for construction, and what parts you will be doing yourself. You tell them that you are just providing the idea or rough sketch of the house, nothing else. No construction company, architect, civil engineer, or laborers are going to work with an arrangement like that. The construction company can just build a house themselves; they don't need your idea; they have plenty of their own.

This is what I experience when I talk with many non-tech wannabe founders. They always complain that it is very hard to find a cofounder to work with.

You need to be clear about what you are going to bring to the table. That is the first step. It does not have to be money. As mentioned in chapter 12 about how to pivot your startup or business, do a stocktake of your assets and strengths.

It doesn't have to be just money. Of course, if you have financial liquidity, it helps, and you have more options. But, it is not the be-all and the end-all.

Do a stocktake of your skills, strengths, and assets. You need to work out where you can add value.

Whether you are looking for a business to join as an employee, or looking for a cofounder to build a startup together, this principle applies.

> *"Knowing yourself is the*
> *beginning of all wisdom."*
> *– Aristotle*

You might be rich in time or experience or have skills that other people need. For example, you are skilled at negotiating, or you are a powerful public speaker.

There might be people out there who need your skills, your experience, wisdom, time, or other resources, and you might need their skills and resources.

The number one way to pivot when you don't have money is to form partnerships. If you want to build a startup, then look for people with complementary skills. Or, if you want to pivot your career, then look for the companies you can add value to in the desired direction of your pivot.

Start with the mirror

In Japan, for over a millennia, the Imperial Treasure was handed down from one emperor to another. This tradition still continues to this day. In May

2019, Japan celebrated the ascension ceremony of Emperor Naruhito. At the ceremony, he was handed the Imperial Regalia of Japan. This Imperial Regalia is said to contain three things: the sword Kusanagi no Tsurugi, the mirror Yata no Kagami, and the jewel Yasakani no Magatama. They represent the three primary virtues: valor (the sword), wisdom (the mirror), and benevolence (the jewel). Not many people, apart from the emperor of Japan, have seen these treasures, and their existence is always surrounded by folklore.

The Sword and the Jewel might seem like worthy treasure for an Emperor. But what about the mirror? Mirrors in ancient Japan represented truth because they merely reflect what is shown to them. Also, mirrors stand for introspection. And knowing yourself is one of the highest forms of wisdom.

Before you pivot, the first thing you need to do is know yourself. If you are going to spend the time and energy in changing the direction of your career or company, then spend some time planning first to get it right.

After you know where you stand, what your strengths and weaknesses are, then as the next step, start looking to form partnerships.

Looking for partnerships

It is quite likely that you do not have all the resources you need to pivot. You feel like you are stuck between a rock and a hard place. But there might be other companies or individuals out there who feel just like you and could use your skills and resources.

When forming partnerships, always have a long term view. Build partnerships that last long term. If you have deep relationships, then when things aren't going 100% smoothly, they'll give you a chance to fix things and learn from the situation. In any new relationship, there is a lot of learning and adjustment that needs to happen. And that is true also in a relationship between two businesses, or a boss and employee.

Catch-22

After I sold my nutraceutical company, I wanted to go back into tech. It wasn't easy to make that pivot for me. Every job that I applied for, I got rejected, partly because I was a business owner for 7–8 years. Every employer thought that because I had been an entrepreneur most of my working life, I would find it hard to adjust to being an employee. Nearly every startup I applied to, I had the same problem.

Be ready for an experience like mine if you are planning to pivot your career. You can end up in the Catch-22 situation, for example; the new employers all say that you do not have enough experience, that's why they cannot hire you. And you are unable to get relevant experience because no one is giving you a chance without relevant experience.

How did I overcome my Catch-22 situation?

There is an old saying in Te Reo (Maori language) -

> " *He aha te mea nui o te ao. He tāngata, he tāngata, he tāngata* "

Which means:

> *"What is the most important thing in the world? It is people, it is people, it is people."*

I solved all my Catch-22 situations using this quote. Nearly everything I have in life is because of people. Every job I got or every business I started or pivoted, has been with the help of people. Make connections, online and offline. We humans are social animals. And we trade with people, and communicate with people. Yes, computers, the internet, and machines help us to communicate and trade more efficiently and at scale. But the end goal is still the same. That is, to get in front of the decision-maker. It doesn't matter how you do it, whether it is through social media or snail mail. As soon as you connect with the right people, you get breakthroughs.

Conclusion

If you are planning to pivot your career or business without money, then do a stocktake of all your assets, skills, and strengths. Work out what is lacking that you need to perform your pivot. Then find people or organizations with complementary skills and strengths and partner with them.

At the end of the day, people still control this world. In most cases, humans are still the overwhelming majority of decision-makers. Yes, more and more systems are starting to be driven by algorithms, but there are always people who can override that.

If there is one thing you can take from this chapter, then it is — focus on the people, and everything else will fall in its place.

INNOVATION-LED PIVOT

"I want to put a ding in the universe."
–Steve Jobs

Innovation happens when you change something that is established by introducing new methods, ideas or products. Different people define it in different ways.

If you ask 20 people to define innovation, you are likely to get at least 19 different definitions.

To me, innovation happens when you improve upon something by using your creativity, skill, and ingenuity.

Why does your company need to innovate?

Innovation can act as a catalyst to make your business grow, and can help you adapt in the marketplace.

- Innovation increases productivity.
  When you find new ways of doing things, you are likely to unlock hidden gains in your productivity. And productivity gain is the holy grail that leads to profitability.
- It helps you compete.
  When you think innovatively, it becomes very easy to beat your competition. You just need to put in a little creativity, and you can easily come up with better ways to design products and connect with customers.
- Innovate more than just products.
  Innovation doesn't have to stop with your product; you can also innovate other non-tangible parts of your business or startup. You can innovate the distribution or the marketing.

What would happen to your company if you don't innovate?

Imagine you have a very popular product. You have lots of customers. Every year your company has been making a profit for the last decade. In fact, things are going so well that your company pays out hefty dividends, and takes part in share buybacks. The economy is going well, and your share price has never looked better.

So you decide to keep things going as they are. You do have lots of new competitors, but they are all at the low end of the market. Only young people choose your new competitors' products.

You decide to stick with your existing range of products and services.

Now, three or four years later, your small new competitors have grown in size. They hold a reasonable share of the market because they have technologically novel solutions that are starting to become more popular.

Seeing their success, you decide to jump into this new category. But alas, your brand and products are seen only as champions of the yesteryears. You start spending money copying the new solutions that have sprung out in the last five years. But everyone who wanted a new solution is already a client of your competitor who is more well known in that new category.

Now you are in real trouble, and you have to start selling your silverware (i.e., existing assets). Your share prices start declining over the next 3–5 years as you keep losing market share to the newer companies whose solutions are seen as more innovative and fresh. Eventually, you file for bankruptcy.

This is a script that many once-successful companies follow, time and time again. You can just replace the name with Kodak or Blockbuster or Borders bookstores…

Side effects of innovation

When you innovate successfully, a few things happen. Firstly, your company size changes. In most cases, innovation will lead to long term growth in the size of the company, as you hire more staff, buy more machinery, or have to move to a larger office, etc. In a minority of cases, your company may initially shrink as it cuts off sections of the business that are no longer in demand.

Secondly, your company might look very different. One moment you are selling computers, you added innovation, the next moment you have the world's largest selling phone. Now the majority of your revenue comes from mobile phones. That is what Apple did.

One moment you are shipping DVDs on subscription, you added innovation, then after a while, you discover that you are one of the largest movie studio and TV production companies in the world. That is what happened with Netflix.

This is what I call an innovation-led pivot.

Innovation will lead to a pivot. It won't be an instant pivot. But you have to be ready for a complete pivot as innovating your current company may take you there.

This is not only limited to startups and companies. This also applies to individual human beings. I was applying for jobs, and I was unsuccessful even after sending out hundreds of applications. So I innovated my approach on how I connect with businesses and ended up owning a business.

The more you innovate, the bigger your pivots are likely to be. Many companies didn't end up with innovation because they pivoted. It was actually the other way around. They sincerely wanted to make their product, service, or methods better with the help of innovation. This innovation led them to a completely new way of thinking and solving the problem.

This new way of solving the problem not only landed them a completely new product or service, but also disrupted the existing industry.

Finally, companies and people who innovate and know how to commercialize their innovation will win it all in the long term. Their stock prices will defy gravity. And people who only look at profitability will always wonder how a loss-making company can be valued at 50 times more than a company that is profitable right now.

For example, at the time of writing this in May 2020, Tesla's market cap is worth US$150 Billion. Compare this to GM — $32 Billion, Ford — $19 Billion, Fiat Chrysler — $12 Billion. The combined market cap of these three major car manufacturers in the US is $63B, which is less than half of Tesla. The funny thing is GM, Ford and FCA all returned a profit for the 2019 year; however, Tesla made a loss of US$892 million in 2019.

I don't have to tell anyone about which company is seen as the most innovative. Tesla started as a sports car manufacturer in the early to mid-2000s. But due to continuous innovation, it might end up as the world's largest battery company or a truck manufacturer or the largest energy company the world has ever seen with tens of thousands of chargers around the globe.

This story is not unique to Tesla or the car industry. Regardless of the industry or the person, if you keep innovating, it will lead to a pivot in your business, startup or personal career.

Your ability to pursue continuous innovation will also lead to the generation of immense value to others. Innovation is what drives the human race forward.

In my personal view, long term innovation-led companies will always outperform companies who only worry about the immediate return.

Regardless of what stage you are at in your career, continue to innovate. Yes, it will lead to pivots, embrace the pivots.

You do not want to be selling whale oil in the age of petroleum. You don't want to be the company selling coal when wind and solar energy is cheaper and easier to produce, and in higher demand. And you don't want to be in the business of nuclear energy when we have managed to build a Dyson sphere.

You have to decide which side of the innovation spectrum you want to be on.

Conclusion

Innovation will make your business sustainable in the long term.

You can innovate more than just your product or services. You can also innovate how you distribute or market or your own company's internal systems.

If you choose to invest all your profits and additional resources on innovation, then that innovation will most likely lead to a pivot in your core products and services.

Finally, innovation is not limited to companies, organizations, and startups. You can also innovate your own career.

REASONS TO PIVOT YOUR STARTUP OR BUSINESS WHEN THERE IS NO DOWNTURN

I s there any reason why you should pivot even if there is no recession or downturn?

I have written most of this book from the perspective of a recession and a downturn, because that is when many businesses and career pathways close down. The people involved in those industries need to either pivot or become unemployed.

But you might be reading this book when you are not going through a recession. Everything is in an upswing; unemployment is down, stock markets are up, so are the property prices. Your business is doing well. So why should you even think about pivoting or look at new ways of doing business? The answer is simple — so someone doesn't come and disrupt you.

Are you going to be the disrupter or the disruptee?

Here is a story of two different industry sectors in the USA. On one side, you have the airline industry, and on the other side, it is Amazon.

The five major airlines in the USA — American Airlines (NASDAQ: AAL), Delta Air Lines (NYSE: DAL), United Airlines (NASDAQ: UAL), Southwest Airlines (NYSE: LUV), and Alaska Air — spent a whopping 96% of their free cash flow (FCF) on share buybacks over the past decade. In reality, it varied from 50%–90%, depending on the airline.

So what this means is that when any of the major airlines in the USA had money leftover, they spent it to help out their existing shareholders for the short term. Doing a buyback increases the prices of stocks instantly. Another strategy that these sorts of businesses adopt is to pay out a dividend to existing shareholders. This doesn't make the business future-proof, but keeps the existing shareholders happy. They are now all in trouble as they have nothing to fall back on.

On the other hand, there are companies like Amazon that are worth nearly a trillion dollars. In its

26-year history, Amazon has never once handed out dividends to shareholders, and rarely takes part in share buybacks.

Why? Because Amazon believes in investing in innovation. No company that I know has had bigger pivots than Amazon. Between 1994 and 1998, Amazon was just an online bookseller. Amazon was super successful at selling books online. It had expanded to nearly every state, and also started international expansion to the UK and Canada. Despite its successes, Amazon didn't just stick to books. Today the most profitable unit for Amazon is its cloud computing business. It is very likely that tomorrow it will be another Amazon business making most of the profits. It could be video gaming, financial services, or pharmaceuticals.

To me, when a CEO decides to pay out dividends or perform buybacks, he or she is saying: "I don't know where to invest this money, and we won't innovate for the future or pivot to another industry, so just take this money."

Going back to airlines. They are not in the business of just selling tickets for people and transporting cargo. They are in the destination business. Helping people and things get from A to B.

How will people do that in the future? We don't know. The airline's choice is to wait for something new in the future, like Tesla's Hyperloop, to come and disrupt their business, or to innovate, and find new methods of getting people from A to B.

To make sure you don't end up like most of the US-based airlines, here are five times you should pivot, even when you are not in a recession or downturn.

- People don't like your product.

  If you have a product and no one likes your product, then it is a clear sign that it is time to pivot. You might even have good revenue and profitability. That's why it is easy to get complacent. Your customers might be using your service or product only because there are no good alternatives.

  For example, when asked, most people don't like airlines and the experience of flying in economy class. You just need to go to YouTube and look at how standup comedians describe their experience of flying on long haul flights. Maybe airlines should invest in completely overhauling the flying experience when they have the funds. Maybe an uber for the air model or maybe something completely different. Disrupt your own industry instead of handing out money for the short term.

- You are relying on heavy marketing.

There is another time when you should look at how you can pivot. It is when you are super successful, your customer numbers are growing, and every day new people are trying your product.

But this growth is purely based on your startup's intense marketing spend fueled by Venture Capital money.

For example, you have a new B2B SaaS startup. You are adding new users in most markets you are advertising. But your LTV (Lifetime Value) of your clients is slightly less than CAC (Customer Acquisition Cost). You have been able to sustain this charade just because you have VC (Venture Capital) funding.

If you are in such a situation, then it is time you have a look at pivoting your product, so you can deliver PLG (Product Led Growth).

Product Led Growth (PLG) is "a go-to-market strategy that relies on product usage as the primary driver of acquisition, conversion and expansion." The principle is that as users gain value from interacting with a product, they will begin to weave it into the way they operate day-to-day.

- Too much yogababble
Yogababble is a term coined by NYU Professor Scott Galloway. It refers to spiritual-sounding language used by companies to sell products or make their brand more compelling on an emotional level. What brands and companies end up with is airy-fairy taglines that don't mean much to the end consumer. They do this to impress and attract funding. Prof Galloway argues that sometimes companies hide behind yogababble to conceal their lack of innovation.

For example, some startups and businesses have mission statements that are filled with hubris like this:

"Elevate world consciousness"
"unleash the world's creative energy"
"transform the lives of people"

The first example is actually the real mission statement of WeWork. Most of WeWork's business is focused around coworking offices and real estate.

To me, if you need to hide behind Yogababble, then maybe you should be looking at pivoting and chasing real innovation.

- You only compete by pricing.

Another key thing to watch is that the only way you compete in your industry is by pricing. You have no other Unique Selling Point.

Whether you are a person, startup, or an established enterprise, you do not want to participate in the race to the bottom.

You might be making revenue right now, but eventually, there will be someone in some part of the world ready to work for less than you.

That's why you need to differentiate or innovate and pivot. As you read in the previous chapter, real innovation leads to a pivot in the long term.

So if you do not have any USPs (unique selling points), it might be time to follow an innovation-led pivot approach.

Conclusion

It makes sense to pivot or look for different ways of doing business when you are in an extreme downturn, and nothing that you do seems to be working. However, it is equally important to follow the innovation-led pivot route when times are good.

You should especially look at innovation-led pivot when:

- People don't like your product.
- You are relying on heavy marketing.
- Too much yogababble.
- You only compete by pricing.

SUMMARY

D ue to Covid-19, there are major interruptions to business and personal life. Most of the people I know are under immense amounts of stress. There is a massive amount of uncertainty. Many businesses are struggling or on the verge of complete collapse. Fresh graduates and young professionals are worried about their career prospects.

But there is a silver lining.

Every recession or downturn forces people to think outside the box. Numerous successful companies are born during recessions or times of disruption. Pandemics, Recessions, Depressions, War, and major natural calamities have happened throughout the past.

And every time our planet goes through such a major event, it brings forth a whole range of disruptions.

These disruptions, in turn, give rise to new professions, businesses, and ways of living.

The Covid-19 situation is going to disrupt how things are done. It will present you with a choice — pivot, adapt, and prosper or resist change, struggle, and perish.

Fight the fear

It is natural to feel fearful or anxious in times of change and disruption. Remember that this too shall pass. Use the OLEG system to Pivot and Adapt your business or career to the new environment. Surround yourself with optimists, understand your limitations, and work only on what you have the power to change. Accept that everything is ephemeral, and this tough time shall pass. Finally, set goals that you can convert into habits.

What is a Pivot.

A pivot is a change in direction or tactics to reach your ultimate long-term goal. When you pivot at the right time, it can be extremely advantageous to your career, business, or startup. You can pivot your product or service by changing what you offer, who you offer it to, or the industry you operate in.

The most powerful pivots happen when you find your purpose and vision.

Don't underestimate the value of persisting

Great entrepreneurs have focus, and they stick to their vision. Even though they might pivot the approach they take to their goal, their character oozes grit and perseverance in moments of adversity. They get things done regardless of the odds they are facing. It might not be exactly as they initially envisioned, but their formidable character helps them get through.

Awesome entrepreneurs have the wisdom to know when they should persist or pivot.

You should persist and not pivot if people love your product and continue to use it regardless of the changing business environment. You should also persist if your idea is going to change humanity forever, or finally, if it is for something that is more than just financial success.

Adopt the contrarian approach

Most businesses continue doing what has worked. Especially if their business has been stable to continuing to grow. This is the correct approach if we lived in a static world where nothing ever changes — fashion never changes, languages never change, laws never change, technology and social norms never change — then you can just do what has always worked in the past. However, we live in an ever-changing world, where everything is in a constant state of flux. We need to constantly adapt to the ever-changing world, so we do not end up like the dinosaurs, such as Blockbuster and Kodak.

Pivot yourself before external disruption forces you to; by that time, it could be too late. Be the business that disrupts itself before others disrupt it.

Pivots are not limited to just startups

Economic and technological change is unstoppable. Individuals, corporates, organizations, and governments all have to pivot at times and adapt to changing environments. Countries like New Zealand have had to pivot multiple times in their short history to adapt to the changing political, economic, and technological landscape.

This economic disruption could be a blessing in disguise. Regardless of whether you are a person, company, state, or a country, if you embrace this opportunity to pivot and find new niches, then, in the long run, you will end up in a much better situation than you were before.

Pivot your career

Pivoting and changing your career is not something you do instantly or as a result of a knee jerk reaction.

Most career pivots happen over time. As people navigate their way through their education, jobs, businesses, and life, they forge a unique pathway for their own careers.

When you are pivoting your career, do not just follow your passion, and watch out for the sunk cost fallacy.

If your career is disrupted or you think it will be disrupted, then do the following to pivot your career.

- Find something at the cross-section of your skillset and interests.
- Look for something in an industry that is adjacent to yours.
- Ask yourself what problems you can solve.
- Make yourself obsolete.
- Find a side gig or volunteer to try new things.
- Upskill and learn new skills online.

High risk - High reward

Most people pivot their careers slowly, or their expertise evolves over time. However, there are some people who completely overhaul their life. They do a complete U-turn.

Pivoting your career or whole life is one of the hardest things you can imagine. Because not only are you changing your profession, in many cases, you might also change your city, friends, daily routine, and more. This sort of drastic change can take you to some dark places mentally. However, if you are successful, then you end up creating a life that is beautiful, purposeful, and fulfilling. Scores of successful people have pivoted their life completely, and they haven't let things like location and age get in their way.

How to pivot your business

Before you think about pivoting, make it your goal to delight your customers. If your product or service no longer does that, then it is time to relook at your offering and pivoting.

To pivot your startup or business:

- Be willing and open to pivot.
- Look at your assets and strengths.
- Hope for the best, but prepare for the worst.

- Act on it fast.
- Communicate effectively and be transparent with your decision.
- Test - Iterate - Test.
- Spend time with positive people and train yourself to spot opportunities.

Pivoting with limited financial resources

If you are planning to pivot your career or business without money, then do a stocktake of all your assets, skills, and strengths. Work out what is lacking that you need to perform your pivot. Then find people or organizations with complementary skills and strengths and partner with them.

At the end of the day, people still control this world. In most cases, humans are still the overwhelming majority of decision-makers. Yes, more and more systems are starting to be driven by algorithms, but there are always people who can override that.

If there is one thing you can take from this chapter, then it is — focus on the people, and everything else will fall into place.

Let innovation lead your pivot

Innovation will make your business sustainable in the long term.

You can innovate more than just your product or services. You can also innovate how you distribute, or market, or your own company's internal systems.

If you choose to invest all your profits and additional resources in innovation, then that innovation will most likely lead to a pivot in your core products and services.

Finally, innovation is not limited to companies, organizations, and startups. You can also innovate your own career.

Innovate and pivot even when there is no downturn

It makes sense to pivot or look for different ways of doing business when you are in an extreme downturn, and nothing that you do seems to be working. However, it is equally important to follow the innovation-led pivot route when times are good.

You should especially look at innovation-led pivot when:

- People don't like your product.

- You are relying on heavy marketing.
- Too much yogababble.
- You only compete by pricing.

Now that you know how to pivot your career, startup or established business. Use all the tools this book has equipped you with.

Go forth, innovate, pivot, and adapt to this disruption and emerge a winner!

ACKNOWLEDGEMENTS

A big thank you to you, the entrepreneur, the young professional, the startup founder, the manager of a corporate, the student looking for a job, and the person owning or working in a small business.

Thank you for continuing your hard work despite the odds. Thank you for persisting. Thank you for continuing to pivot and find new ways of doing things. Thank you for trying, failing, and getting back up. Thank you for making this world a better place.

Keep going! Keep innovating! Keep building! Keep caring!

This book is for you.

Here is a quote from Theodore Roosevelt that sums it up for me.

> *"It is not the critic who counts; not the man who points out how the strong man stumbles, or where the doer of*

deeds could have done them better. The credit belongs to the man who is actually in the arena, whose face is marred by dust and sweat and blood; who strives valiantly; who errs, who comes short again and again, because there is no effort without error and shortcoming; but who does actually strive to do the deeds; who knows great enthusiasms, the great devotions; who spends himself in a worthy cause; who at the best knows in the end the triumph of high achievement, and who at the worst, if he fails, at least fails while daring greatly, so that his place shall never be with those cold and timid souls who neither know victory nor defeat."

- Theodore Roosevelt

Kia Kaha! (Maori for "be strong, keep going")

REFERENCES

Who is this book for

1. Everything is terrible

2. Overcoming this downturn
https://medium.com/swlh/13-massive-companies-
that-started-during-a-recession-ba769e38d0ad
https://www.businessinsider.com/sheryl-sandberg-
coronavirus-pandemic-interview-facebook-2020-3?r=
AU&IR=T

3. Losing Control
https://www.psychologytoday.com/nz/blog/what-
would-aristotle-do/201105/the-fear-losing-control

4. What is a Pivot?
https://www.dailymail.co.uk/health/article-5134761/
A-cure-curse-JOHN-NAISH-wonder-sex-drug.html

5. Should you Persist instead of Pivoting?
https://www.youtube.com/watch?v=D56QeyyQMLI

https://www.today.com/health/humans-new-york-
project-raises-3-8-million-fight-pediatric-t94501
https://www.ted.com/talks/angela_lee_duckworth_
grit_the_power_of_passion_and_perseverance
https://teara.govt.nz/en/map/9184/bar-tailed-
godwits-
migration-route

6. Reasons not to pivot
https://www.brainyquote.com/authors/michael-
jordan-quotes

7. Contrarian approach to business
https://www.statista.com/statistics/277061/kodaks-
global-revenue-since-2005/

8. Examples of Successful Startup Pivots
a. Burbn
b. Tune in, Hook up
https://www.cnet.com/news/
youtube-started-as-an-online-dating-site/
https://www.youtube.com/watch?v=
jNQXAC9IVRw
https://www.telegraph.co.uk/news/uknews/
1584230/Web-could-collapse-as-video-demand-
soars.html
https://en.wikipedia.org/wiki/Bandwidth_
(computing)

c. Tote
https://www.businessinsider.com.au/pinterest-ben-silbermann-building-company-2018-10?r=US&IR=T
https://www.fastcompany.com/3001984/pinterest-pivot
https://www.stern.nyu.edu/experience-stern/about/departments-centers-initiatives/centers-of-research/berkley-center/programs/venture-competitions/past-winners/2008-2009

9. When a Country Pivots
http://www.export.ac.nz/
newzealandstradehistory.html
https://teara.govt.nz/en/overseas-trade-policy/page-4
https://en.wikipedia.org/wiki/Economic_history_of_New_Zealand
https://www.stuff.co.nz/business/farming/116439723/have-ewe-herd-nz-is-down-to-fewer-than-six-sheep-per-person
https://usatoday30.usatoday.com/marketplace/ibi/dubai.htm

10. Pivoting your Career
http://news.bbc.co.uk/2/hi/business/3515287.stm

11. Pivoting your Life.
https://tim.blog/2018/06/18/brandon-stanton-humans-of-new-york/

https://www.inc.com/business-insider/people-who-found-success-and-changed-careers-after-30-years-old.html

12. Pivoting your Startup or Business
https://bigthink.com/personal-growth/stockdale-paradox-confronting-reality-vital-success

13. Pivoting with no money
https://en.wikipedia.org/wiki/Imperial_Regalia_of_Japan

14. Innovation-led Pivot
https://nz.finance.yahoo.com/

15. Reasons to Pivot your Startup or Business when there is no downturn
https://www.nasdaq.com/articles/airlines-didnt-waste-all-their-cash-flow-on-share-buybacks%3A-american-airlines-did-2020-03
https://www.bloomberg.com/news/articles/2020-03-16/u-s-airlines-spent-96-of-free-cash-flow-on-buybacks-chart
https://www.visualcapitalist.com/breaking-amazon-makes-money/

ABOUT AUTHOR
SAM KAMANI

Sam lives in Auckland, New Zealand, with his wife and two energetic sons (6 and 4 years old). He loves spending time with his family, camping, hiking, kayaking, playing tennis, table tennis, and multiplayer games on Xbox.

Sam is an author, speaker, and entrepreneur. "The 30 Day Startup" - the first book co-authored by Sam - was an instant hit and often trends at number one on Amazon in its category. Sam is currently the CEO and Cofounder of ProductDone. ProductDone helps entrepreneurs and founders bring their tech startup ideas to life. Since graduating in Computer Science, Sam has worked in three continents, and before starting ProductDone, was working with startups in New Zealand and Silicon Valley. He is a frequent speaker at business events and on podcasts. He has advised both startups and established businesses in innovation and growth strategy.

Sam is also currently working as cofounder with a small team to gamify finance. His team is building a unique new platform that merges Esports and financial trading. You can find out more about it here — Ensydr.com. You can follow all Sam's updates on Linkedin - linkedin.com/in/samkamani/ or twitter @ samkamani

www.ingramcontent.com/pod-product-compliance
Lightning Source LLC
Chambersburg PA
CBHW070931210326
41520CB00021B/6882